Election Insiders

Behind the Scenes with the People Who Make Your Vote Count

D1248670

Election
Insiders

Behind the Scenes with the People Who Make Your Vote Count

Gloria Shur Bilchik

gatekeeper press
Where Authors are Family

Columbus, Ohio

ISBN (paperback): 9781642379532
eISBN: 9781642379549

Cover Design: Eva Bochem-Shur
Interior Book Design: Peggy Nehmen

Printed in the United States of America.

Published by Gatekeeper Press
2167 Stringtown Rd., Suite 109
Columbus, OH 43123-2989
GatekeeperPress.com

CONTENTS

1

What You Don't See Matters

"Voting is a fundamental political right,
because it is preservative of all rights."
—*US Supreme Court,*
Yick Wo v. Hopkins (1886)

QUITE POSSIBLY, A MINIMUM-WAGE maintenance worker wielding a Dustbuster could have changed American history. Could have. But, unfortunately, didn't.

After the hanging-chad debacle of the 2000 presidential election, researchers swooped in to figure out how voting had gone so terribly wrong. In an exhaustive post-mortem study of the punch-card voting equipment in use in Florida at the time, election guru Douglas Jones of the University of Iowa concluded that the problem may have been "chad jams." Underneath the platform into which voters inserted their punch cards, clumps of chads—small pieces of paper—had piled up, leftovers from previous elections. They prevented the stylus from fully perforating the ballots, creating the "dimpled," "hanging," and "pregnant" chads that turned vote counting into a nightmare. Jones's ultimate recommendation was embarrassingly basic: Vacuum out the residue regularly.

Lesson learned: Behind the scenes in elections, things that happen or, in the case of Florida in 2000, things that don't happen—big things and little things—things that voters never see, don't think about, and may not even imagine—make a difference.

Voting is the essential, democracy-defining act of citizenship, yet most of us have scant knowledge of its under-the-hood mechanics. Voters see the public-facing side of elections—the poll workers, the voting machines, the ballots, the campaigners outside polling places—but those elements, among others, are just the top line. Even the most engaged voters can be unaware of—or even badly misinformed about—what happens beneath the surface to make elections tick.

With elections under attack from foreign intruders—specifically Russia and maybe China, as well—it's more important than ever to understand the underpinnings of elections, so that we know what's needed to keep it all from unraveling. Counter-intelligence agents and IT experts get the bulk of the glory and airtime in the critical effort to keep our elections free and fair, and they deserve the attention. They are shining a light on attacks that too many people in positions of power would rather deny, tacitly support, or even overtly solicit.

But there's even more to safeguarding US elections than fighting off the cyber-attacks that get the headlines. Behind the scenes in the county or township where you vote, there's a whole other world of election workers—democracy defenders—whose jobs are invisible to most voters but of equal consequence. Who are they? What do they do? And why do they do it?

The job titles of these warriors—clerk, supervisor, site manager—don't say much about what they do. But while the generic titles and bland bullet points of their job descriptions may not spell it out, everything these election insiders do is part of an implicitly understood election-security effort. It's just not the part that you hear about very much because, unfortunately, security has come to be narrowly defined, in everyday parlance and news reports, as cyber-security. In fact, it is much broader than that.

Much of what protects our elections consists of backstage grunt work—an endless cycle of processing voter registrations, making arrangements for polling places, figuring out how to implement new laws and regulations, drawing maps, answering voters' questions, keeping track of expenditures, vacuuming out the chads (now out of style, thankfully), packing and unpacking election day materials, and a myriad of other tasks that are outside of most voters' fields of vision. Elections are only as good as the people who run them.

"But what do you do the other 364 days of the year," is every election manager's least-favorite, but probably most frequently asked question. If there's one thing that election administrators want the public to know, it's that they have full-time jobs, even in "off" years. "That's why they call them election cycles," said a manager in my local jurisdiction. "For us, the next election starts as soon as the last one is over."

No matter what their job, everyone you see working on election day, as well as the phalanx of others operating out of public view, is in one way or another, a security guard. Obviously, elections involve a lot of rules. These workers live and breathe them, doing the sometimes rewarding, but often maddeningly detailed work that helps hold our democracy together. They measure success by how smoothly things run and by the voting public's acceptance of the results of the election. "The ideal election day," one worker told me, "is one that is so uneventful that we are completely bored."

Job titles and descriptions vary from election office to election office, from county to county, and from state to state—as do workloads. Some are better at their jobs than others. Everybody makes mistakes. They're not all heroes. Some tolerate the job just for the paycheck—usually not a very large one, it should be noted—and many don't stick around for long. But it's probably safe to say that most of the people who stay in these jobs—some for decades—do their work with a collective goal of making elections go right. These behind-the-scenes democracy defenders, and the jobs they do, are the focus of this book.

▪

"Elections are approximations, and a certain amount of confusion, error, malfunction, and even fraud inevitably creeps into far-flung and myriad polling places," wrote journalist David Von Drehle in a 2010 *Time* article. "Voters ignore or misinterpret instructions. Volunteer poll workers misapply rules. Machines fail, sometimes in subtle ways that aren't noticed." It takes a big effort—even in small jurisdictions—to keep it all together.

For elections to be perceived as meaningful exercises worthy of our participation, voters need to sense that the game is on the up and up. We want to be certain not only that our votes are tamper proof and our personal data protected, but also that the election structure itself is fair, with reasonable rules properly and equitably enforced. We want convenient polling places and hours of operation. We expect to be recognized as eligible to vote when we show up and to know that people who don't qualify can't game the system. We want to be confident that our votes will be recorded as intended and that they will be counted—exactly once. Is that too much to ask? Of course not. In Australia, voting is mandatory. Non-voters can be fined up to eighty Australian dollars for not participating, and the result is, typically, a 90 percent turnout. In the United States, we encourage voting, celebrate it with "I Voted" stickers, and beat up our collective self over low turnouts and other people's lack of information about candidates and issues. However, as a nation, we're not very good at following through on our own patriotic exhortations about the importance and benefits of voting. While voter turnout has risen in recent election cycles, we're still topping out at a less-than-stellar 60 percent, and that was for the high-impact 2016 presidential election. In the November 2018 midterms, voter turnout was between 50.3 and 53.4 percent of the citizen voting-age population, depending on whose statistics are cited. That was the highest rate for a midterm election since 1914, but still a rather dismal number, considering what was at stake. As Thomas Jefferson once commented, "We do not have government by the majority. We have government by the majority who participate."

Americans don't vote for a vast variety of reasons. One of them, unfortunately, is distrust. We like to call ourselves "the greatest democracy in the world," but underneath that veneer, for many people, there is an underbelly of doubt in the system. Some of these misgivings are justified, spawned by people who make headlines by perverting the process. Some are the result of deliberate disinformation and propaganda. But a significant portion comes from nothing more than a lack of knowledge of how things work. And, of course, cynicism and partisanship play a role, too: Democrats accuse Republicans of skewing the vote by suppressing voters. Republicans accuse Democrats of trying to register people who shouldn't be allowed to vote. Third parties and independents complain of being unfairly excluded from the system or forced to jump through extra hoops to get on the ballot. A large swath of eligible voters hears it all and decides to abstain, calling the whole thing a rigged system in which their votes don't count, anyway. Why bother?

For those who do bother, many begin to wonder about election operations only on election day itself, and often only when things appear to be going wrong. We are, to an alarming extent, election blind. Former British Prime Minister Tony Blair once said, "The single hardest thing for a practising [sic] politician to understand is that most people, most of the time, don't give politics a first thought all day long. Or if they do, it is with a sigh ... before going back to worrying about the kids, the parents, the mortgage, the boss, their friends, their weight, their health, sex and rock 'n' roll ... For most normal people, politics is a distant, occasionally irritating fog."

Elections are not magic. But they are, in my view, rather wondrous, in the same way that US Postal Service workers are amazing in their ability to—for the vast majority of mailings—take an envelope with an address and a stamp and get it to its intended destination. Most of us don't know how they do it, but it works. Voting is like that, too. We show up at a polling place, or we fill out a mail-in ballot. Our vote gets recorded. We end up with a credibly elected government and a peaceful transfer of power. I am in awe of how well the system works—even with its many undeniable flaws.

■

Just before the November 2018 midterm elections, I accompanied a group of high school students on a backstage tour of our local election board's headquarters. Our tour guide was Eric Fey, one of the top administrators. He took us into places most people never get to see. We got a glimpse of workers sorting voter registration cards, checking signatures on petitions, and getting equipment ready for election day. Those two hours gave me a tantalizing taste of what goes on out of public view and sparked my curiosity. That tour also helped me realize that a case study in election management was right in my own back yard.

Everyone lives in an election jurisdiction—the official term for the local government entity that oversees elections. In the United States, there are about 8,000 of them. Among the tiniest is Petroleum County, Montana, with 364 registered voters. The largest is Los Angeles County, with nearly five million voters. Most are small, with a median of 2,000 registered voters. In fact, a third of the local election jurisdictions in the United States are small towns or counties with very few staffers dedicated to elections. But overall, larger jurisdictions—meaning, generally, those encompassing more than 50,000 registered voters—serve most of the national population. Regardless of the size of the jurisdiction, many election challenges are universal, and keeping elections secure is a shared, top priority.

I live and vote in St. Louis County, Missouri, which has the biggest election operation in the state, with about 750,000 registered voters, 400 polling places, and 3,000 election-day workers to manage. It ranks among the twenty-five to thirty largest jurisdictions in the nation, and it is my base of operations for this book.

Over the past eighteen months, I've met with scores of workers at the election office, learning about their responsibilities and observing them on the job. I reviewed documents, attended public meetings, sat in on training sessions, worked as an official election judge, and hovered around headquarters on several election days. My goal has been to try to understand the intricacies of jobs we voters know very little about, to gain insight into the challenges, and to get a sense of how this work fits into the overall picture of keeping elections fair.

My research took me into areas I did not know existed. And as I learned about how elections worked in St. Louis County, I began to see parallels to similar jobs, processes, and unexpected occurrences elsewhere. I had stumbled into a microcosm of the American election world. And while the project began locally, in the end, it led me far afield. Interspersed throughout this narrative, you will find many anecdotes, news stories, and election oddities from around the US. These stories help prove not only that no two election jurisdictions are alike, but also that despite their differences, they share many issues, from mundane to hair-raising.

Obviously, using my home election district as my base of operations is not a random or scientifically determined choice. It's familiar and convenient. But it turns out that it offers a fair example of the essential principles at play in most election offices around the country. Importantly, under current leadership, St. Louis County's election board has earned a reputation in election circles as forward-thinking, well managed, and focused on being increasingly professional rather than partisan. Its leaders and workers have experienced the full range of ups and downs. The things that keep them awake at night would be instantly recognizable to people with similar jobs in other communities. Certainly, some other election districts are more familiar to the general public—such as Palm Beach County, Florida, for its confusing "butterfly" ballots in the 2000 presidential election, and Cook County, Illinois, where early twentieth century ballot-box stuffing was legendary. Their names stick in our collective memory because they've gained attention as a result of a headline-making screwup, or an incident or pattern of corruption. You don't hear as much about the ones that mostly get it right.

I can't say with any authority that St. Louis County's Board of Elections is the best election-management operation in the nation. There's no government-sponsored rating system. But measured against recommendations issued by the most influential election-focused organizations, such as the federal Election Assistance Commission (EAC), St. Louis County looks pretty good. It has stayed out of the public-shame spotlight, essentially, by doing a very respectable job, while coping with occasional missteps, flawed policies, and near catastrophes that have instilled some painful lessons.

Election security requires constant vigilance. Even a cursory review of headlines from around the country makes it obvious that elections can be thrown into doubt and voter confidence undermined, not just by cyberprobes from Russia or China, but also by intentional, partisan-driven procedures and personnel decisions. Sometimes, as the horror-movie cliché goes, the call is coming from inside the house.

My take on St. Louis County's election insiders is that their intention is to scrupulously maintain the guardrails and stay alert to potential threats and procedural pitfalls. They seem to be trying to get it right. But that's a conclusion I'll have to leave to you.

▪

I'm not pretending that this book is a comprehensive, statistically driven dissertation on election security or the American way of voting. Such a project is far above my pay grade and limited expertise. I'll leave that to academicians, statisticians, political analysts, and historians who have already tackled that daunting task. Their work offers important source material for this project.

Nor have I written an exposé of the dirty tricks that political operatives and corrupt officials employ to try to swing elections their way. I'm more interested in rightdoing than wrongdoing. But I'm not naïve: Bad things happen—both innocently and intentionally, and I have included many examples in my reporting. What I have learned, as a result of going behind the scenes, is that there are many fronts in the effort to ensure the fairness and security of American elections. I hope that I have provided some useful information about the effort—sometimes out of sight, but often in plain view—that goes into making elections work.

▪

When I first approached the St. Louis County Board of Elections about this project, leaders of the management team, to their credit, got my intention immediately and were ready to welcome me in to see how things work and to interview employees. I began our first meeting by asking, "What do you wish the public knew about what you do here?" That question hit home, apparently, because in the first five minutes, the stories began to pour out. It helped, I think, that few people had ever asked.

It took a little longer to convince the governing board of commissioners, who—rightly—were more cautious about admitting a total stranger into a place where the privacy of voting and voters' information is sacrosanct. But as I attended public meetings and began to become a familiar face around headquarters, doors began to open. I went in not knowing what I was about to find, but I was committed to reporting what presented itself. They never denied a legitimate request for documents or information. Human beings answered the phone, and managers and employees regularly returned calls and replied to emails and texts. Everyone was patient when I asked basic questions or didn't know things I probably should have. They talked candidly about some harrowing crises and reminisced about the crazy circumstances and oddities that crop up in the life of an election worker.

They put no restrictions on what I asked employees. I don't think they gave away any secrets, because there are very few secrets in the organization—by law. I didn't get any special favors, no insider whistleblower information, usually not even a heads-up on public meetings, equipment demonstrations, training or test runs. They assured me that everything was posted on their website and social media, and that's where I got my notifications, just like anyone else in the general public would.

I had no idea that an ordinary citizen could have access to some of the documents and information I reviewed, just by asking. I can't attest to this level of openness in other jurisdictions, but I hope that others operate at a similar degree of transparency. That would further shore up my faith that our fragmented, fragile election system is—with some exceptions, of course—in the hands of people who want to do the right thing.

▪

We have come a long way from the early days of American voting, when colonial citizens gathered in the town square on election day and, one by one, stood up to declare their votes out loud—a procedure known as *viva voce*. Back then, a ballot was something that a voter might write out by hand or tear out of a newspaper ad published by a candidate and bring to a polling place.

It's tempting to be nostalgic for those quaint, seemingly innocent times, but in truth, election mishaps and deliberate attempts to rig elections are a longstanding American political tradition. Rules created by the Founding Fathers made voting available to only about 6 percent of Americans—white male property owners of a certain age. In one colony, vote buying was so rampant that the practice acquired the nickname, "Rhode Island-ism." Later, in the 1880s, political campaigners were known to buy votes and then, to make sure that the voter actually cast the ballot for the intended candidate, required ballots to be deposited into a clear box where the vote could be seen—a flagrant violation of our ostensibly sacred, secret-ballot tradition. "Apparently, ballot fraud was so common, it developed its own vocabulary," according to an article in *Smithsonian Magazine*. Party bosses bought voters and organized them into "colonizers, who moved *en masse* to turn the voting tide in doubtful wards. 'Floaters' flitted like honeybees, wafting from party to party, casting ballots in response to the highest bidder. 'Repeaters' voted early, and sometimes in disguise, often."

Those antique forms of cheating would be hard to pull off today. But the lessons learned from historical instances of election chicanery live on. Many of the jobs and procedures now in place in an election jurisdiction near you evolved in response to the shocking variety of ways that politicians, elected officials, political parties, voters, and other players have attempted to gain unfair advantage in elections. How well these safeguards work is essentially in the hands of the people backstage.

Here are some of their stories.

2

"A Failure of Elections 101"

In Crawford County, Kansas, results from five of the county's 16 polling locations were accidentally counted twice. Some precincts reported a turnout of 110 percent. "The mistake was not mechanical. It was human error," said the county clerk.

–Pittsburg KS Morning Sun, *November 9, 2018.*

"WE'RE OUT OF BALLOTS," said the panicked poll worker on the other end of the phone line. That's how Eric Fey's worst day as director of elections for St. Louis County, Missouri, began. And that was only the first of many similarly frantic calls on April 5, 2016, when St. Louis County was conducting its annual elections for mayors, city councilpersons, and other officials, both countywide and within its ninety-three municipalities. The calls started coming in at 8 a.m., just two hours after the polls opened, and the problem cascaded through the rest of the day. By poll-closing time at 7 p.m., 62 polling places, out of 431, had either run out of paper ballots or had experienced worrying shortages. It was a nightmare scenario—a potentially career-ending fiasco—the kind that any election administrator would dread. Running out of ballots is the *Titanic* of election-day disasters.

Talking about that day—even after nearly four years—is still painful for those who went through it. As I interviewed people, I momentarily hesitated to ask about it. I knew that it was among the darkest days in Fey's work life—and that of those around him. It damaged the election board's reputation. It shook the confidence of many voters. And it provided convenient fodder for heat-seeking members of the media, as well as for election-conspiracy theorists. But it merits examination as a prime example of what can happen when even the most carefully constructed election safeguards break down.

As calls came in, Christian Tolbert, an assistant director at the time, checked his spreadsheets and scratched his head in confusion, because the number of ballots that precincts said they had received didn't jibe with the numbers he thought had been distributed. But there was no time to stop to figure out what had gone wrong. It was Def-Con 1, Code Red. By any measure of urgency, it ranked at the highest level of election-day problems. Voters were being turned away. Poll workers had no experience with this situation. The integrity of the entire election was in jeopardy. The only saving grace—and at the time, it certainly didn't feel that there was one—was that this was an April election, not a high-stakes November presidential contest.

Fey and his staff went into full-on triage mode. "My first thought, honestly, was that this was the day that I was going to lose my job," Fey told me. He had good reason to expect that he was about to get the axe. His immediate predecessor had been embroiled in her own ballot-shortage fiasco in 2014. She was fired three weeks before Fey took over as director in 2015. At the time, he was thirty-two years old, making him one of the youngest full-time election directors in the country. "I quickly realized that I had to get over that personal fear, for the moment, put my head down, and focus on fixing the problem."

Tolbert hijacked an information-technology intern, and together they created clean spreadsheets on which they recorded who needed what. Tolbert and others dashed to the on-site storage area to see if, among the surplus stacked there, they had the ballots they needed for specific precincts. Fey dispatched anybody available to be a runner, driving boxes of ballots to the undersupplied polling places, or shuttling to the off-site printer's warehouse, where there was more overstock. Fey and his staff also answered calls from justifiably irate voters and fielded questions from reporters in hot pursuit of a potential election scandal.

"You don't have time to ask, 'Where did we go wrong?'" said Tolbert. "You have to put the fire out now. We had people running all over the place for ballots. It was so scary because our county is so large. You just can't get around that fast. And no matter what you do, it's not good enough, because you feel you should have been prepared beforehand."

The problems at the polls stoked a crisis of confidence and spurred legal action—a sure sign that public opinion of the election operation was spiraling downward. As the mistakes reverberated through the day, attorneys representing the election board, a voter, a candidate, and the treasurer of a ballot issue sought a court order to keep the polls open at problem precincts for an extra two hours. A St. Louis County judge rejected the request, but another judge granted an appeal. Unfortunately, the court's decision came after the polls closed, when many of the workers had already left. As a remedy, voters got permission to cast their ballots after closing time at election headquarters.

Reportedly, about ten voters did that, but the damage, in the minds of some voters, was already done. Officialdom expressed its strong displeasure, too. Missouri's governor called the debacle "completely unacceptable" and called for an investigation.

"My biggest fear in general about elections are the things that we haven't even thought about," said Fey, who prefers to refer to disaster-prevention measures by a more technocratic name: risk mitigation. "Every election, something happens that you could not ever have imagined."

Some of those unforeseen, but suddenly all too real, events can be of an organization's own making, like the St. Louis County ballot-distribution fiasco. The most infamous self-inflicted election disaster in recent memory was the 2000 presidential election, when hanging chads and butterfly ballots in Florida confounded voters, election officials, and the courts—and resulted in the election being decided by the US Supreme Court. The damage to public confidence in elections still resonates two decades later.

Perhaps as a result of the 2000 election debacle, even the most minor, local—and accidental—aberrations from the expected routine can make voters question the validity of what they are experiencing. In Alabama in November 2018, voting slowed to a crawl because some machines couldn't scan paper ballots, after humidity in the area where they had been stored pre-election caused the paper to swell. In Chicago, voters reported receiving only one page of the two-page ballot they were expecting. In St. Louis County itself, an exceptionally long ballot, necessitated by a complicated election, exceeded scanners' capability, causing some machines to spit them back at voters. In each of these cases, disgruntled voters were quick to claim voter suppression.

Another way to mess up election day is by forgetting to include power cords in polling-place set-up kits, as happened in Gwinnett County, Georgia, where voting machines had to run on batteries that ran out of juice before the end of the day. A similar power-cord foul-up caused a one-hour shutdown of the lone voting machine at an elementary school in Michigan. Officials later discovered that, although the machine was plugged in to a surge protector/power cord, it ran out of power after two hours. After much consternation by election officials, a sharp-eyed school custodian found the problem and flipped the power switch to the correct setting: On.

Not having enough ballots, obviously, is a much more serious system breach that undermines the most fundamental building block of American democracy. The St. Louis County mishap was not an isolated incident. In August 2018, voters in many precincts in Michigan's Oakland County showed up to vote, only to be told, "Sorry, we're out of ballots." In that case, a voter-turnout tsunami had swamped election officials' expectations, and they were caught short.

A similar problem occurred in Prince Georges County, Maryland, where at least 5 percent of precincts experienced a ballot shortage, causing thousands of voters to be stuck in line for hours. The election office jumped into action, sending out about two hundred more paper ballots to each of those polling sites, but rainy weather and rush-hour traffic delayed their arrival. "That is never going to happen again," elections administrator Alisha Alexander vowed in an interview on WTOP-TV.

At one precinct in Sarasota County, Florida, for more than an hour after polls opened, voters couldn't cast ballots because there weren't any, and they were told to either vote at Sarasota County election headquarters or to come back later in the day. Some poll workers erroneously instructed them to vote at a nearby precinct. The problem occurred in just one precinct, but that didn't make it any less troubling for individual voters, who were, at least, temporarily inconvenienced and, at worst, disenfranchised.

In the aftermath of Michigan's missing-ballot problem, the American Civil Liberties Union summed up the impact of issues like these, stating, "Whatever the reason, the problem constituted a scandalous potential infringement of voting rights."

Equally egregious was the situation that blew up in Hartford, Connecticut, in November 2014. Early-morning voters at some polling places couldn't cast ballots, because the voters' lists—essential to checking off registered voters as they come in—were AWOL. "It was a failure of Elections 101," one official told the *Hartford Courant*. Connecticut's secretary of state filed a complaint against the Hartford registrars for "gross misconduct."

Hartford's mayor characterized election mishaps as a threat to social equality. "We have a city that is very poor economically," she told the newspaper. "We have a lot of poverty in our city. The one thing that our residents have which is of equal wealth to anyone else in this state is their vote, and we need to protect that."

■

Anything can happen, and it does. With more than eight thousand election jurisdictions in the United States, election-day crises are probably inevitable. Some are beyond human control, but nevertheless, require a response to ensure the integrity of the election and a plan to deal with similar emergencies in the future. Natural disasters figure significantly into the worries and planning in election offices. Election administrators scramble when monsoon rains flood streets, when hurricanes hit, and when squirrels chew through power lines, knocking out voting machines and communications.

In March 2017, in New Hampshire, a record-setting blizzard dumped more than fifteen inches of snow on election day—locally known as town meeting day. Election officials had a difficult choice to make—one that would balance the right to vote on schedule against the possibility of voters getting injured on snow-packed roads and in treacherous parking lots, versus the state's election laws, which turned out to be unclear. "It was not a trivial decision," one town official said in a news report.

Then, buried under the snow, one-third of New Hampshire towns delayed their elections for two days—a move of questionable legality that left some officials worried about possible prosecution. Their anxiety was justified: New Hampshire's secretary of state asserted that town officials had no legal authority to change election dates. "The law says you follow the political calendar," he said. State statutes define the second Tuesday in March as town election day. "If there's any dispute, this is the law."

▪

By closing time on that now infamous April 2016 election day in St. Louis County, Eric Fey was exhausted and emotionally wrung out. As co-director, he did the right thing, owning the problem and taking the blame for the mistakes. He appeared on local TV news broadcasts and publicly apologized.

"I would like the voters of St. Louis County to know that I have an absolute passion for this job," said Fey in a *mea culpa* interview with St. Louis Public Radio. "I love election administration. I observe elections around the world. I attend conferences. I'm a voracious reader on the topic. And I want to make this office the best election authority in the state of Missouri and a model for the rest of the country. Yesterday was a huge setback in that regard. And rebuilding the credibility of this office is going to be a long, uphill slog."

That night, Fey called one of his mentors in the election-administration community and tearfully apologized for letting him down and failing in the mission—a cause that had evolved into a life purpose and become a virtual part of Fey's DNA.

An after-action investigation into the ballot mix-up revealed that it was the result of both a database error and human fallibility. Somewhere along the line, numbers in the election board's data matrix had been mistyped, or transposed, or both, creating a critical error in merging versions of the database that allocated ballots. No one noticed the problem, even though proofreading the print order is a built-in backstop for every election. So, some precincts got too many ballots. Some got too few. It was a data-manipulation mistake reminiscent of snafus that happen in corporate offices everywhere, only this one had the effect of throwing an election into chaos, with potentially disastrous consequences.

But it could have been even worse. As serious as the problem was, the ballot shortages did not, in the end, affect the outcome of the elections, so there was no need for the worst-case scenario—a do-over. But it took a while for everyone to recover, and the memories still burn.

No one lost their job, but there were consequences. Fey's Republican counterpart retired. One observer told me that the board of commissioners felt a need to send a stern rebuke that would essentially say, "Look, you need to reassess what's going on here." They suspended Fey without pay for two weeks, and an assistant director for one. That hurt. It's an episode in Fey's otherwise well-respected work life that he'd rather not rehash. "I never want to be on CNN again," he remarked when I asked him about it.

▪

The minute-by-minute details of the April 2016 election debacle have begun to blur, but the scars remain. Following the incident, the governing board issued a fiat that remains tattooed on the brains of everyone in the department: "We will never run out of ballots again." That dictum would, in fact, play a major role in a huge decision that the department would make three years later.

For St. Louis County, the ballot-shortage nightmare was a low moment, one that would make any election official cringe and take an extra-close second look at procedures in their own bailiwick. Its impact goes to an intangible factor that election researchers call "societal security," meaning public confidence that election results are accurate and the belief that voting is an important part of our democracy.

Fey earned a reprieve. Then, feeling that he still had things to accomplish in pursuit of the Holy Grail of democracy— the flawless election—Fey picked himself up, undoubtedly humbled, and went back to work to get ready for whatever new, unpredictable challenges were lurking in the next election cycle. Like Fey, election administrators everywhere fear the unknown, create firewalls where they can, but ultimately must manage the realities. A good solution to one crisis does not inoculate them against the next. They live in a Murphy's Law world. They go to conferences and hear the horror stories told by their peers, and they try to learn from them, but the election playbook can't anticipate everything, even when it is updated regularly.

"Every election is a practice run for the next," said Fey. And in the grand scheme of things, his terrible, heart-pounding election day in April 2016 was just another day—an especially tough day—in the life of the mostly unseen people in charge of elections. The question is: With the obvious stresses of election work, with the stakes so high, and with the probability that if something goes wrong, they will get the blame, who takes these jobs, and why do they do it?

The answer is complicated.

3

The Accidental Profession

James Allen was sworn in as the new city clerk for Bloomfield, Alabama, on December 16, 2019. He resigned on December 30, prior to beginning the job. "I have dealt with an unexpected weight of anxiety that I have been unable to overcome," he said. He apologized for not realizing that he could not handle being in a public position.

—Downtown Newsmagazine,
January 3, 2020

MOST PEOPLE WHO GET into the business of running elections arrive serendipitously and have little understanding of what is about to hit them. Eric Fey calls election administration the accidental profession. "Nobody wakes up on their sixth birthday and says, in their little first-grade voice, 'When I grow up, I want to be an election administrator,'" said Fey, still in his job in 2019, with his reputation intact after surviving the debacle of April 2016.

People who take the top jobs have a variety of titles embossed on their business cards, including secretary of state, lieutenant governor, registrar, or county clerk, to name just a few. For Fey, the job focuses one hundred percent on elections. But that's not the case everywhere. In New England states, the person in charge often is the town clerk, whose duties may include supervising elections as well as maintaining real estate records, signing death certificates, and issuing dog licenses. Texas election clerks also approve cattle brands. But whatever the title, in the wake of well-documented foreign election interference into US elections, the stakes for people in these positions are higher than ever.

According to the EAC, today's typical local election official is female, white, and has a college degree. Fifty percent of people who run elections have worked in the job for ten or more years. Overall, the election-management world is populated by skilled, seasoned professionals. But there is no standard way to get the job of election chief, and there are no universal rules for how to do the work.

Federal laws govern the dates and the underlying rules for presidential, congressional, and senatorial elections, but it's up to the states to decide who runs those elections, as well as state and local contests within their boundaries. Adding to this crazy-quilt system is further decentralization of election responsibility within many states themselves, where authority rests with counties and townships. A state legislature may pass the election laws, and a secretary of state may enforce them, but implementation—and often interpretation—is up to local election managers. They become what some election scholars call "street-level bureaucrats" who live in the real world of election operations. The day-to-day procedures they create and the workarounds they devise out of the necessity of their special circumstances can make voting a very different experience state-to-state and county-to-county, with vastly varied levels of security.

The American election system is a mishmash. But in terms of safeguarding elections, that may be a good thing—even if it's unintended. In a televised interview in 2019, former FBI Director James Comey put it this way: "The good news for all of us is that our election machinery is a total hairball, and there is comfort in that. It's decentralized. It's some nice old lady putting a voting machine under a basketball hoop. It's not connected to the internet. It's very hard to attack. I don't feel worried about that."

Decentralization has its pros and cons. The National Conference of State Legislatures (NCSL) devotes a significant portion of its description of state election structures to this issue:

> Critics say the level of local control can lead to mismanagement and inconsistent application of the law. This often comes into focus in large federal elections especially, when the media and the public focus on how different the voting experience can be depending on where a voter lives.
>
> On the other hand, this decentralization allows individual jurisdictions to experiment and innovate—to see how elections might best be run for the state and the locality's particular circumstances.
>
> The dispersed responsibility for running elections also makes it extremely difficult, if not impossible, to rig US elections at the national level. It also holds authorities in local jurisdictions accountable for the management of their own elections, so if something goes wrong, citizens can go directly to their local government rather than blame problems on the distant federal government.

The career path to becoming a top election administrator varies. Seventy percent of US election administrators are required by state and local laws to run for the office, which can mean refereeing elections in which they themselves are candidates—a situation that's unique to the United States. But electing the top election officer can be problematic for voter confidence, especially when the election chief is running for higher office and, essentially, overseeing their own election. In 2018, three secretaries of state ran for governor in their respective states, while retaining their authority over all aspects of statewide elections.

One of them was Kansas Secretary of State Kris Kobach, who ran for governor. In the August primary, he led by just 121 votes after the initial count, triggering a recount that Kobach had the authority to supervise. He insisted that overseeing the recount in his own election was not a problem. Ultimately, he won the nomination but lost in the general election, despite having previously implemented draconian voter ID regulations that could potentially limit voting by his political opponents.

Still, the situation is troubling. "The conflict of interest is extreme, and the best course of action is for the secretary to recuse from all decisions involving the counting of votes, recounts, and any further legal or administrative action. No person should be a judge of his or her own case," said Rick Hasen, an election-law expert at the University of California, Irvine School of Law.

Another structure is the board of commissioners' model, used in nine states, as well as in St. Louis County, five other Missouri election jurisdictions, and other localities as well—although, given the fragmentation of America's election structure, it's hard to nail down a number. In some states, the governor appoints the board and, in many cases, picks an equal number of Republicans and Democrats to fill the seats. In St. Louis County, there are just four commissioners. That's an unusual, but brilliant, configuration, current board chairman, Sharon Buchanan-McClure told me. "How many four-person boards do you know of? The even number of members creates an insulation so that no one person can manipulate how elections are going to be run."

The commissioners hire the top administrators and are the ultimate missionkeepers. "Our responsibility is to conduct accurate, efficient, timely and fair elections. And by fair elections, I mean assuring that everyone who has the right to vote has that opportunity, and that we protect the system from abuse," said Buchanan-McClure, speaking in the lofty mission-based language you'd expect of a board chairperson. At board meetings, she is an authoritative presence. But she's far from a stick-in-the-mud. In 2011, she appeared with her husband, the CEO of a large corporation, as a disguised worker on TV's "Undercover Boss." On a more serious note, Buchanan-McClure honed her view of civic responsibility through a career steeped in public-affairs jobs. Civic engagement is a family tradition. Her grandfather was an election official when Theodore Roosevelt ran for President on the Bull Moose ticket in 1912.

Buchanan-McClure and the board leave day-to-day operations to the professional administrative staff. One current board member, Matthew Potter, straddles both worlds. For five years, he was a hands-on administrator at the nearby St. Louis City election board. That's an unusual resume point that gives him a unique perspective.

The board meets formally once a month, year-round, even in "off" years. They faithfully follow the familiar *Robert's Rules of Order* agenda used, almost universally, from corporate board-rooms to student council meetings. Someone must take notes for the record, and that job often falls to Hannah Talley, Eric Fey's administrative assistant. During meetings, she sits primly in a cramped corner, hurriedly transcribing minutes on her laptop computer and drafting on-the-spot motions synthesized from rapid-fire discussions among commissioners and staff. "They're talking a mile-a-minute, back-and-forth, so I have to be tuned in all the time," she told me. "Usually, there's two of us taking notes, so whatever I miss, the other person can help me fill in. It's important to get it right."

Peggy Barnhart joined the board in 2017, bringing along relevant insight from her career as director of communications for the local chapter of the American Red Cross. "It's not a crushing amount of work for us, but we do prepare in advance, and we take our jobs seriously," she said. "The staff does a great job, every day, but oversight is essential. We sometimes see things that the staff doesn't."

These commissioners are quick to point out that they're not a rubber-stamp, window-dressing advisory board larded with glittery names that look good on the letterhead. They're engaged. They ask tough questions and push for fact-based answers. Their deliberate approach can be frustrating to administrators who do the day-to-day work and who just want to get the job done. The big decisions don't happen without the commissioners' approval, and they don't give it automatically. During a year of attending public board sessions, I sensed that the relationship was, overall, cordial and collegial. At one meeting, though, I witnessed a surprisingly contentious clash. "That was a rough one," a staffer told me, sounding bruised the day after the dustup. But by the next meeting, the tension appeared to have dissipated.

Commissioners can be hands-on, too. Buchanan-McClure, Barnhart, and Trudi McCollum Foushee, a lawyer who has been on the board since 2015, make a point of visiting polling places on election day, to observe the ground-level consequences of their decisions. In a special election in November 2019, their itinerary took them to eleven sites. For their efforts as commissioners, they receive a stipend of about $600 per month. They're not in this for the money.

■

Unfortunately, some election offices around the country are notorious for being political dumping grounds. An open secret in many jurisdictions is that, whether the title is registrar of voters or sheriff, the job can be a political plum handed out as a favor to a party loyalist or to a big donor with zero experience in running elections.

In the early 2000s, a local newspaper in Florida's Broward County reported that the county's chief election official hired "a perpetually drunk, homeless man, who didn't open and time stamp nearly three hundred absentee ballots. The ballots were later found buried in a filing cabinet. Considered too unsteady to drive to the post office and often absent, he was occasionally reprimanded but never fired. He could not be fired, a government employee later explained during legal deposition, because of his friendship with the election director." Later, as a result of this and other incidents, the election director was sacked and was marched out of the office accompanied by Broward County sheriff's deputies.

That's a particularly outrageous example. But while American elections cannot yet be deemed free of political cronyism, in more recent years, the trend in enlightened districts has been away from political patronage and more toward professionalization. That's not to say that political connections don't play a part. They do, but often as a networking advantage rather than as evidence of corruption.

Case in point: Eric Fey. He got his start in elections when he was an undergraduate in college. As a way of picking up spending money, he signed on to be an election-day poll worker, a fourteen-hour shift that paid, at the time, about $120 for the entire day. That job fit nicely into his major in political science, if not into a long-term wealth plan. After graduating, he got a full-time, lower-level job at the election board. He stayed for three years.

Dick Bauer was the beloved-by-all assistant director of elections when Fey came in for an interview for that first job. "He was a natural," Bauer told me. "Hire this guy now," he told his boss. Bauer remained a Fey fan and friend, even ten years after retiring from election administration. He called Fey "a person who lives and breathes elections."

Some people who stumble into this kind of job try it on for a while and then move on or flee. Then there are people like Eric Fey. "It just sort of happens. It gets into your blood," said Fey, now thirty-six years old.

In South Dakota, Sue Ganie knows what he means. She's the auditor for Fall River and Oglala Lakota counties. "I applied for the job as an elections clerk in 1983—I wasn't even registered to vote yet—but I got the job and eventually moved through the ranks," she said, when interviewed by the National Association of Election Officials a few years ago. "I never thought it would be a lifetime career."

In St. Louis County, Fey earned a master's degree in public administration, but only because there are no degree programs in election administration in the United States. The University of Minnesota was the first to offer a professional certificate in election administration. Others have since jumped in. Aspiring administrators need twelve to fifteen credits, depending on which program they enroll in, to get the piece of paper to frame and hang in their offices. Also, several election-focused associations offer popular short courses, some of them online, zeroing in on specific aspects of elections. You can take three-credit-hour courses called "Elections and the Law," "Strategic Management of Election Administration," or "Poll Workers: Recruitment, Training and Retention," among others. But if you're seeking a PhD, a master's, or even a bachelor's degree in elections, you're out of luck.

Early on, when Fey tried to advance in the election department, higher-ups rebuffed him. His master's degree didn't qualify him for the job, they said. You need real-world political experience, they advised him. So, he left the department, got a job as a top aide to a Democratic member of the St. Louis County Council, earned a reputation for intelligence and hard work—and made those requisite political connections as well. Then, one day in late January 2015, when the then election director lost her job, the board tapped Fey for the position.

Talking with Fey and observing his interactions with coworkers at election headquarters, I was impressed by his affability and low-key demeanor in a job that, as that 2016 election-day debacle demonstrates, has a virtually zero margin for error. His vague resemblance to actor John Krasinski, who played Jim Halpert in the TV series "The Office," adds a halo of humor and puckishness. I witnessed a bit of that one election day, when he wheeled a cart full of materials into the office, chanting in a mock stadium-food-vendor voice, "Peanuts, popcorn, Crackerjacks." Those traits—all of them, not just the Jim-from-"The Office" look—clearly serve him well.

His own office reflects his love of all things election, not only in St. Louis County but internationally as well. In recent years, he has visited a variety of countries as an official election observer. Framed sample ballots collected from Sri Lanka, Moldova, Russia, Kyrgyzstan, Macedonia, Ukraine, and Uzbekistan add flair to his office décor.

"To be good at this job, you have to love it—all of it, all of the challenges and ups and downs," he told me. "You'd better stay cool under pressure. You need to manage a lot of people. And you're always looking around the corner for the next wrinkle. I've learned to live with a high level of uncertainty."

Fey told me that a speaker at a conference he attended described election administration as one of the five most stressful jobs in the professional world. Election director doesn't officially rank in the top five, but if it does compare with the high-stress jobs typically at the top—firefighters, police officers, enlisted military personnel, airline pilots, and event coordinators—it clearly qualifies as very intense. "In a way, also, it's like managing a big project at NASA," said Fey. "But unlike at NASA, when big problems arise in an election, there's no scrubbing the launch."

One afternoon, as I awaited a meeting at election headquarters in St. Louis County, I struck up a conversation with Rob Wiebusch, the man sitting next to me. He told me that his job as senior sales manager for a national voting-machine vendor has put him at ground zero in multiple election jurisdictions around the country. He has observed many administrators in their native habitat. He happened to have been at St. Louis County headquarters during the 2016 ballot-shortage crisis, and he was drafted as an emergency ballot delivery guy for the day.

"The job of election director reminds me of a circus performer," he volunteered. "It's the guy who has multiple spinning plates on long sticks. He has to keep them spinning, and as one slows down, he spins it to keep it going, keeping them all balanced, and moving back and forth from one plate to another. Just when one looks like it's going to stop spinning and fall, he saves it. And then he adds even more. You're left marveling at how they do it."

∎

Eric Fey's origin story of building a resume for the job by combining relevant education and practical political experience is somewhat atypical. More often, election administrators have backgrounds as lower-level elected officials or political-party loyalists—or both.

Fey's current Republican counterpart at election headquarters is Rick Stream, whose path fits that more political history perfectly—but in a good way. He started this job in 2017, after many years in the thick of local and state politics. Stream shares the title of director of elections with Fey, not just because it takes two people to manage the operation but also because in St. Louis County, everything about elections must be bipartisan.

"Every function requires a Republican and a Democrat," Fey explained to me. "You need an R and a D to open the door to the tabulation room. You need an R and a D to approve every absentee ballot. You need an R and a D to check voters' IDs at every polling place. The only thing you can do here by yourself is go to the bathroom."

That's not true everywhere. St. Louis County is one of only six jurisdictions in Missouri large enough to require a bipartisan structure under state guidelines. Across the country, party balance in election offices is not that common. Of course, political bias—real or perceived—in election operations is a major cause of voter distrust. But the reality is that in many jurisdictions—particularly in rural areas, but in some urban areas as well—party balance is a pipe dream. One party is so dominant in the voting population that there simply aren't enough people from the minority to go around.

Some election experts have been pushing for a completely different structure. Among them is Amber McReynolds, formerly director of elections in Denver, Colorado, and now head of Vote at Home. She favors a non-partisan election-management structure. "At the local level, the officers, if they are elected—and many of them are—should not be partisans," she told me. "That means that the party should not be nominating the candidates. Under a non-partisan structure, you get on the ballot by petitioning. There's no R or D next to your name on the ballot. Not being accountable to a political party is a key transparency issue." McReynolds also favors choosing election chiefs in odd-year elections. "That way, they're not running for office while they're trying to run the big midterm or presidential elections in an even year."

In St. Louis County, Rick Stream describes the election director's job as having the scope of a CEO and many of the elements of that job level, but with a public-service and in-the-trenches twist. "The CEO factor means that you're planning the strategy, discussing overarching ideas, and directing subordinates who are over other people to do this and that," said Stream—a lifetime non-drinker in a job that has been known to drive other people to overindulge. "But normal CEOs in the corporate world don't look at the details nearly as much as election leadership needs to."

When Stream was contemplating taking this job, he sought the advice of legendary former election director Paul DeGregorio, now a nationally known elections expert, whose tenure in St. Louis County in the late 1980s and early 1990s had a transformative effect—for the better, I've been told—on the department. "Paul told me, 'Rick, when you get there, remember it's all about the details, the details, the details, the details. You have to pay attention to details, even at your level.' If you mess up on the details, that's when the election goes haywire," said Stream. "His advice has stuck with me."

So, Stream and Fey are constantly code-switching between the high-level strategizing of CEOs and the mundane aspects of overseeing the day-to-day operations of the office. They're in charge of personnel as well as all the technology, processes, and procedures essential to running elections. He and Fey do a lot of managing by walking around. "You've got to be out on the floor, talking to people and seeing for yourself what's going on," said Stream.

It's easy to visualize him doing that. Looking like a television casting director's vision of a white-haired, stately CEO, Stream comes across as a good-natured, calm and competent, grandfatherly kind of guy, fully equipped with natural people skills, honed over many years as a politician. If a sense of humor helps in the job, he's in good shape. Just before one board meeting convened late in 2019, he displayed a gift from an office worker—a basket filled with bags of salty snacks, accompanied by a t-shirt that read, "I'm just here for the food."

On a more idealistic level, Stream described the mission behind his job as striving for the flawless election. "That's our goal, to run elections perfectly—even though they never are—with professionalism and expertise, so that the voter can get in, get out in a timely fashion," he says. "And it's more than just technically making sure that happens. Obviously, we have to do that. But we have to convince the public through our words and also through what they see when they're voting. We want voters to say, 'Hey, I have confidence that this is being done right.'"

His earliest brush with elections came when he was seven years old. He fondly remembers walking with his mother up and down neighborhood streets in south St. Louis County, knocking on doors to drum up votes for Dwight Eisenhower in the 1956 presidential election. You hear a lot of stories like that from people with careers in election management. Moms who drag their kids around on campaigns and take them along to vote apparently have a lasting impact. Later, Stream accrued years of political experience as he ran for his local school board—and won four times—and then for Missouri state representative, a position he held for four terms, until he was term-limited out. In 2015, he ran for St. Louis County executive, but lost by a narrow margin.

Some politicians who move into election administration turn out to be little more than hacks: They enjoy the title and the paycheck, but not the work. Paul DeGregorio—decidedly not a hack—encountered that mentality as soon as he took over as St. Louis County election director in 1985. "On my first day,

I found the person who was to be my secretary. I inherited her from the previous administration," he told me. "She took me to a file cabinet and opened a drawer. 'This is what we do around here on Fridays,' she proudly announced to me, with a wink and a smile. It was a drawer full of booze. That was one of the first changes I made. I got rid of all of it."

Unlike that long-gone secretary, Rick Stream takes his job very seriously. During his political career, he was vice-chairman of Missouri's House Budget Committee, so he knows his way around money. That skill adds value in an organization that depends on the county for its operating budget.

Surprisingly, Stream, who has been around elections for most of his seventy years, came into the job with very little knowledge of the inner workings. Like many other election administrators around the country, he learned on the job. As a candidate and officeholder, he'd interacted with election head-quarters many times—as a customer. He dutifully voted, of course. He knew the rudiments of being a candidate, such as the deadline for filing to run for office, the election schedule, and the boundaries of his district. He regularly came into the election office and waited at the customer-service counter while staff brought out the precinct maps that he asked for. But like the rest of us in the general voting population, he'd never been behind the scenes, and he had no idea about the processes or the people that made it all happen.

"I didn't know how complex it was to run elections," he said. "I didn't know all the departments. I didn't know about having to train all the poll workers, how much training was involved there, the warehouse situation, all the machines, IT, the tabulation room, the ballot room. I didn't understand any of that."

The high anxiety of making big-news elections work, and the drudge work of post-election mop-up are the bookends of a job that few voters understand, he said. "A lot of people think we don't do very much between elections. In fact, two weeks after we finish certifying an election, we start on the next one. We're always planning for the next election, and that involves everyone and every process we have, no matter how small the election. Even in years with light schedules, we're busy."

A look at St. Louis County's 2019 election calendar supported that assertion. Stream and Fey started the odd-numbered year with only the annual April municipal elections on the books. Then, everything changed: Several special elections to fill vacated positions popped up, transforming an initially slack-looking year into something more intense.

That ever-expanding, ever-evolving election calendar is a feature—not a bug—of American democracy. The world of elections is a perpetual-motion merry-go-round. Elections never stop. They have immovable deadlines. And that, we should remind ourselves, is a good thing, even if it complicates the job of election administration—even if it's hard to keep track of—because it keeps the wheels of democracy greased and rolling.

The inevitability of the next election is a fact of life, whether a manager is running a huge jurisdiction or a tiny one. It's possible that where you vote, it's a one- or two-person show, where if you walked into the office, the person in charge might recognize you and, like a regular at TV's "Cheers" bar, know your name. Some county clerks administer elections for fewer than one hundred voters. But that's far from typical. Only about a third of local election jurisdictions in the United States are small towns or counties where the election chief can visit and supervise every polling place. By comparison, to make elections work for its 750,000 registered voters, St. Louis County needs sixty to sixty-five full-time, year-round staff. Cook County Illinois, with 1.5 million registered voters, employs 130 full-timers and sends out 15,000 temporary workers to staff polling places for big elections.

In many towns and counties, the election department is the smallest local government agency for most of the year, but it balloons with temporary workers to become the biggest on election day. To supervise that many people, in that many places, in that short a span of time, election administrators need some big-league management skills.

"Funny you should mention that," said Fey, when I asked for a peek at his department's organizational chart early in 2019. "We just updated it." As these charts go, it's rather simple, with straight-line relationships and clear divisions of labor that even an outsider can understand. A *D* or an *R* follows every name in each section—visual confirmation that there's bipartisan balance. Overall, the structure gives a sense of transparency and accountability that are valuable characteristics in a locally run, taxpayer-funded organization, especially the one with the huge responsibility of making elections work.

But while competence is obviously critical at the top echelons of an election office, a lot also depends on the skill and dedication to the mission of people whose titles and names appear in the lower sections of the chart.

Just below Stream and Fey in the hierarchy are deputy directors Julie Leicht and Christian Tolbert. As one might expect, they oversee more of the day-to-day aspects of the department, including personnel, finance, purchasing, mapping, pollworker recruitment and training, information technology, voter registration, absentee voting, and the thousands of details and problems their subordinates encounter and dump in their laps when all else fails.

Leicht landed in election administration after an extensive career in public service—both in government agencies and in the nonprofit world. "I come from a political family," she told me. "My aunt and uncle were state representatives, and I grew up working in campaigns. You know, when they would have the fire truck going through the subdivisions? I was the one throwing out the candy to the kids. So, politics has always been in my blood, and I just find it fascinating." But even with her extensive resume of public-sector jobs, she walked into her first day in the election realm with very little knowledge of how it all fit together.

Tolbert's is a work-your-way-up story. Twenty-five years ago, his college career—funded by a wrestling scholarship—came to an end when, in a budget crunch, his school cut his sport from the roster. He lost the scholarship, but he has kept the wiry build and purposeful demeanor that undoubtedly served him well on the mat.

A friend of a political friend suggested that he apply for a job at the election board. He started in the warehouse and stayed for many years. But he used those years well. "I tried to learn as much as I could about all the departments, to kind of become a jack of all trades. I figured, while I'm here, it's not just a job. I'm going to do the best I can so I can become an asset," he said. He had a knack for fixing things and a wrestler's skill for problem solving, and, while he wouldn't call his rise in the department meteoric, he advanced steadily. Now, as deputy director, one of his responsibilities is overseeing his old stomping grounds in the warehouse—an area that, in 2019, would play a central role in the future of elections in St. Louis County. During one of our conversations, he proudly mentioned that he had just completed the remaining credits for his long-interrupted bachelor's degree.

■

Fey, Stream, Leicht, and Tolbert are the higher-ups with the offices that have doors and a view of the outside world. But to get real insight into what goes on behind your ballot, it helps to know a bit about both the top-level jobs and the ones that live in the boxes several steps farther down on the organizational chart. In St. Louis County, the titles aren't very descriptive: clerk, senior clerk, supervisor, assistant director, etc. But the jobs are real, performed day in and day out by people who do the detailed, often repetitive, unsung grunt work that we voters rarely think or ask about.

In St. Louis County, everyone, including the top executives, works in a plain-vanilla office that occupies a chunk of what once was the Northwest Plaza shopping mall, now repurposed as an office park. A few managers have offices. The rest of the crew works in a bullpen with half-wall dividers separating different areas. Part-timers and temps hired during peak election periods work at tables crammed into any available space—sometimes in the warehouse.

My journey into these back-office spaces began with the people who draw the lines that drive virtually every aspect of an election.

4

The Mapping Guys

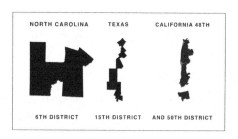

NORTH CAROLINA   TEXAS   CALIFORNIA 48TH

6TH DISTRICT   15TH DISTRICT   AND 50TH DISTRICT

To illustrate the absurdity of gerrymandering, Ben Doessel and James Lee of the advertising firm Leo Burnett created a font they named "Ugly Gerry." Each letter approximates a US congressional district that has been drawn to favor a single political party.

ROB RYAN GRADUATED FROM college with an unusual major: geography. As he walked across the stage to receive his diploma, as one of just seventeen geography majors at the University of Missouri in 2013, he had no idea that a few years later, he'd be working behind the scenes in election management. Like many of us, he didn't realize that elections depend on maps. It turns out that maps are the conceptual infrastructure that underlies much of a voter's experience on election day: who we can vote for, where we vote, which issues appear on our ballots, and even how long the lines at our polling places might be. Nothing happens in an election without maps. Bad maps make bad elections.

Coworkers in the St. Louis County elections office fondly refer to Ryan and his counterparts, Bill Hartnett and Matt McLaughlin, as "the mapping guys." In election management—a line of work that attracts its fair share of detail-obsessed people—the work done by the mapping guys could be deemed "nerdy." But they don't seem embarrassed by that characterization.

Their official titles are mapping coordinators. Much rests on their work, and they know it. Ryan proudly notes that he's an Eagle Scout—which I interpret as shorthand for being serious, responsible, achievement and service oriented, and an eager beaver. He looks and acts the part: young, tall, positive, engaging, occasionally cracking wise. It's not a stretch to envision him in his khaki uniform, with all his badges sewn in tidy rows on the Eagle Scout sash.

Ryan found his way into the realm of elections like many others—by happenstance. He previously worked for what he calls "a short minute" as a temp at a parks agency and then for a commercial mapping company. Neither job excited him. When a few years into his career, he heard about the election-mapping job he jumped in, immediately recognizing that the mission was a great fit, even though he knew very little about elections. "My knowledge consisted of showing up to vote on election day, casting my vote, and going home," he said. "Then I realized that this job means that I get to help people know where they vote. I get to help people know what they vote on. Who they vote for. And I get to be a part of the system that helps that happen." An Eagle Scout answer if ever there was one.

Bill Hartnett is a veteran election worker but newish to the mapping department, with two-plus years under his belt so far. He and Ryan came aboard at about the same time as part of a department effort to modernize. For many years, Hartnett worked election days as a frontline polling-place assistant supervisor, while his day job was in information technology. Becoming a mapping guy meant combining the two worlds. Ryan calls Hartnett an IT whiz—an apt description for an MIT graduate—and credits him with devising some nifty programs that streamline parts of their operation. Hartnett knows the machinations of information technology inside out, and if you let him, he can probably talk IT all day.

Matt McLaughlin was new to the department in 2019. But he's hardly a political newbie, having soaked up election savvy working as a manager for candidates in a variety of campaigns.

The mapping guys share their small, three-desk sector of the office with a large light table and a huge plotter—a specialized printer that churns out oversized maps as well as giant sticky-back sheets used for informational signs at polling places. Mapmaking, of course, occupies much of their time, especially between elections, and particularly in the run-up to elections, when candidates flood the zone with requests for detailed precinct maps of their territories. Sign-making is a sideline, most likely delegated to the mapping department because they're the ones with the oversized plotter.

Municipalities and townships are customers, too. "Local officials call us asking for maps of their boundaries and wards," said Ryan, sounding bemused. "I sometimes think to myself, 'Wait a minute, aren't you guys supposed to be the ones who have that information? You're asking us?' It seems backwards, but it's part of our job."

In election world, mapping means keeping track of—and continuously updating—the boundary lines of precincts and other local voting districts. In St. Louis County, there are a lot of boundary lines to maintain. In fact, the mapping guys of St. Louis County work in one of America's most complicated election jurisdictions.

During one of my early tours of election headquarters, Eric Fey offered a slide-show presentation of the complexity of his county's election map. He started by projecting the overall outline of St. Louis County's 523 square miles. Then, one by one, he added overlays displaying the boundaries of districts that put candidates and issues on the ballot: ninety-three cities, twenty-eight townships, seven County Council districts, twenty-six school districts, forty fire districts, two US congressional districts, seven state senate districts, twenty-nine state representative districts, nine library districts, separate taxing districts for museums, sewers and roads, and more than twelve hundred active voting precincts. As he laid one atop the next, it became clear that many of them overlap, but none share exact boundaries. By the time he was done, the whole stack looked less like a road map and more like a spider's web on steroids.

In any given election, any voting entity in that pile could place a candidate or tax issue—or several—on the ballot. You vote where you live, so the candidates or issues you vote on depend on where you reside in relation to the boundaries of each district. And that is a very big deal because, on election day, everyone needs to vote on the ballot that includes the issues and candidates that pertain to them.

Giving voters the wrong ballot is a major election day no-no. In a 2012 contest for a seat in Missouri's legislature, so many voters received the wrong ballot that the election, which ended with a tiny margin of victory, had to be rerun later. Department veterans still shudder when they remember that incident. The St. Louis County map is a puzzle with thousands of pieces and intersecting boundary lines. "It's so complex that election managers from other cities come here just to see how we handle it," said Ryan. "Administrators from Philadelphia visited us and were shocked." Philadelphia is at the other end of the complexity continuum, with just one school district and one fire district for the entire city, Ryan noted, perhaps with a whiff of jealousy. Closer in complexity are Kansas City, Missouri, which is divided among four counties, and Cook County, Illinois, which contains 29 townships and more than 130 municipalities, some of which are not even completely contained within the county boundary line.

"We have more precincts in Chicago than they do in all of Iowa," Jim Allen, a spokesman for the Chicago Board of Election Commissioners told the *Chicago Tribune* in 2015. "This is a big job."

"Every election jurisdiction has a different odd slice of pie to work with," said Ryan. "That is, if your election office even has a mapping department. A lot of smaller districts don't. Some rely on the county or township planning department, which in many cases is not solely focused on election mapping." Ryan didn't overtly offer an opinion as to whether that configuration is beneficial or not, but election lore contains many stories of wrong ballots and mislabeled precincts that underscore the importance of the mappers' focus and attention to detail.

One key task for an election mapper—again, if there is one—is to make sure all the boundary lines are both accurate and up to date. It sounds like an easy job because cities are cities and townships are townships forever. Not so. The lines can change. Cities sometimes annex additional areas, or even vote themselves out of existence, as several did in St. Louis County in 2018 and 2019, reducing the number of municipalities to eighty-eight. One of them was the now-defunct McKenzie, which encompassed just twelve acres and had a population of 134 at the 2010 census. "They were running their local government out of one of their kitchens, and they just decided that they were done," said Eric Fey.

In addition, school districts sometimes expand their reach, and new taxing districts for roads or community amenities can arise. Any of these can create an altered mapping reality.

"That's when you have to start drawing new lines," explained Hartnett. "You could have a transportation district get born, and it has voters in it, and you have to add it to the map. Or it can be just the opposite: Not long ago, we had a road district dissolve. That meant erasing a layer and rethinking the map."

Most critically, the US Census, held every ten years, can identify population shifts that compel state legislatures to redraw congressional and state legislative district lines. Redistricting is all about maps. Gerrymandering—redistricting's evil twin—is the politically motivated and controversial use of mapping to draw legislative districts skewed toward one political party. That strategy violates the fair-election axiom asserting that honest maps are essential.

Redistricting is normally beyond the scope of county-level election mappers. However, the inevitable changes created by the 2020 census will impact Ryan and others similarly tasked around the country. "Depending on what the census shows, everybody with jobs like ours could be very busy revising maps. And those changes will hit voters and candidates in later elections," said Ryan.

▪

Clearly, mapping elections is a complicated business with real-world consequences. Fortunately for St. Louis County, Ryan has a superpower. He's the resident guru of Geographical Information Systems (GIS), an advanced technology that adds a twenty-first century level of precision to mapmaking. This is not to say that previous mapping guys produced inferior maps. In fact, the level of accuracy of earlier maps is impressive, considering the more limited tools of the trade in earlier times. We've come a very long way from the "There Be Dragons" days of medieval mapmaking, but we still rely on the mapmaker's eye, skill, and judgment to keep us—and in the case of election mapping, our local governments—from falling into the abyss.

"GIS is like Google maps, but with a nice database behind it," Ryan explained, in a GIS-for-Dummies way. "It lets you visualize data very easily and simply. That feature lets you analyze it, and slice into it, and look at information that you can't see in a traditional database format." Many policymakers regard GIS as a foundational technology, and not just in election management. GIS drives a wide variety of important government functions, from locating 911 callers to planning forestry operations.

GIS has gone viral in election offices, and for good reason: Not only does it bring efficiency and precision to mapping and election information, it's a problem solver, and it doesn't take a graduate degree in IT to operate at the data-entry level. Hawaii, Arizona, and Washington have all recently installed voter registration systems that use a GIS-based, address-management tool. Instead of using archaic, and much more limited, street maps and two-dimensional indexes, they're using GIS to more accurately register voters in the proper districts.

One trendsetting use of GIS is playing out in Honolulu, Hawaii, where GIS is helping people without a permanent address register to vote. Honolulu's election administrator uses GIS to assign homeless people a "home address" where they spend nights—even if that is on a park bench or under an overpass, or another non-traditional location. The system registers them with an address point on the map that accurately defines their place of residence. Hawaii is unique, too, in using GIS to track voters displaced, in mandatory evacuations, by lava spewed from the Kilauea volcano. A few years ago, Hawaii election officials used GIS to proactively identify these voters and send them absentee ballots.

On a less dramatic level, another plus of GIS is what it can do to enhance the voter's experience. If you have ever yearned for a sample ballot, GIS is your new Secret Santa. In St. Louis County and in other GIS-equipped areas, you can get much more than a tiny-print list of the contests on the ballot. "Now, voters can go to our website, type in their address and see where they vote, what their ballot will look like, and what's on it—a customized sample ballot," says Ryan. "People really want that. Plus, we now not only give you the address of your polling place, we tell you what door to enter, and what room to go to. We've gone out to all our polling places and taken pictures of the entrances, and that's now on the website, linked to voters' addresses, too. There's also a link to Google maps, to help you find your way. And just recently, we debuted another enhancement: Putting in your address gets you all of the above, plus a complete listing of all of your districts and the names of all of your elected representatives."

▪

Getting the boundaries in the right places and pinpointing where voters live are essential functions, but they're just the starting point. Once they've properly aligned the lines, mappers must read between and beneath them. "Part of our job is to slice and dice the entire county into reasonably sized voting precincts that fit inside the correct boundaries," said Ryan.

Note: A polling place and a precinct are not the same thing. Fans of television shows like "Law and Order" may think of precincts as police headquarters, but that's a different use of the term. Strictly defined, a precinct is a district of a city or town marked out for administrative purposes, such as elections. The word comes from the medieval Latin *precinctum,* meaning enclosure or boundary line.

"Precincts are essentially the puzzle pieces we use to assign voters to polling places," said Hartnett. It's probably safe to say that the mapping guys have at least heard of every street in the county, because their daily task is to manage all the addresses inside the county line and to assign every address to a precinct.

That quasi-encyclopedic knowledge of streets comes in handy. During one election-day observation, I watched and listened as Bill Hartnett, virtually pinned down all day at his workstation, fielded call after call from voters searching for their polling places. He recognized most of the polling places voters were trying to get to because he had a hand in procuring them and pinpointing them on the jurisdiction map. Assisted by GIS and Google maps, Hartnett was able to help them find their way. It was an object lesson in how good data, well visualized and communicated, is an important background factor in making people feel confident that their votes matter.

■

No matter what state you vote in, where you vote depends on many factors, including: where those crisscrossing district boundaries are; how many people live in your precinct and those that are close by; logical lines of demarcation, like rivers or major highways; and the availability of a suitable building that can handle voting traffic. The mapping guys try to make precinct divisions on major roads or natural features of the earth, because those boundaries make sense to people.

"Size matters, too" said Hartnett. "If a precinct is too large or too densely populated, it means that all those voters won't fit at a single polling place, so we may have to change the shape of the precinct." Too many voters mean long lines and disgruntled people. Too few create inefficiencies and wasted resources. According to the US Election Assistance Commission, the median number of voters per polling place in 2016, in large jurisdictions like St. Louis County, was about 1,500. Small districts had about 400 voters per polling place, and medium districts had about 875.

Philadelphia, with one million registered voters, has an inventory of 829 polling places—considerably more than other jurisdictions of similar size. In 2018, City Commissioner Al Schmidt told the *Philadelphia Inquirer* that his mission was to make polling places easy to get to. "I think it's more than average just because we value accessibility and keeping polling places as close to people's homes as possible," he said. "People without physical disabilities are usually able to walk to their polling place."

Sometimes, polling place assignments seem weird, with people who live next to each other voting in different places.

That can happen when boundary lines hit in illogical spots, or when new construction inadvertently straddles the boundaries. Ryan cited the local example of residence halls at Washington University in St. Louis. Apparently, no one consulted with the mapping guys when the university built new apartments on the school's east campus. The building's footprint ended up on both sides of the election-significant dividing line between the City of St. Louis and St. Louis County. "To notify students about registering and voting, we had some sorting out to do," said Ryan. "We ended up having to map, unit by unit in some cases." Rumor has it that some apartments that straddled the line got their city versus county designation by measuring square footage and determining which side most of the apartment was on.

They need to get it right, or things can go terribly wrong for voters. "The worst thing a mapper can do is to put the lines in the wrong place," said Ryan, describing a cautionary tale in which New York City was sued for just such a mistake. "They drew the boundary of a state rep district on the wrong side of an apartment building, putting a statistically significant number of voters in the incorrect precinct. They had to rerun the election based on that screwup."

Even a small error can have a big impact. In 2017, election officials in Newport News, Virginia, learned that lesson the hard way. With the balance of power between Republicans and Democrats in the state legislature up for grabs, a Republican from Newport News won a race for state representative by ten votes. A recount overturned the original result, giving the Democrat a one-vote win. But a court invalidated the recount and ruled the election a tie, forcing officials to settle the election by drawing a slip of paper out of a blue ceramic vase from the Virginia Museum of Fine Arts. The Republican won. Later—too late—the *Washington Post* discovered that twenty-six voters—enough to swing the outcome of the race—had voted in the wrong district because local election officials had assigned them incorrectly, using zip codes as their guide rather than maps.

It's understandable to want to attribute part of the problem to voters who didn't know they were voting in the wrong place and on the wrong ballot and, therefore, didn't call attention to the mistake. Volumes have been written on America's rampant political ignorance—documenting the disturbingly large percentage of voters who don't know the names of their representatives, the districts they live in, or the identities of candidates on their ballots. But the Virginia foul-up had its origins in a mapping mistake, which might have been avoided if local officials had access to the high-level mapping technology available at the state level.

▪

Between elections, when their friends outside election world think they're goofing off, election mapmakers are surprisingly busy. Mapmakers everywhere—and virtually anybody with a full-time job in elections—object to the idea that there is an "off-season." Election mop-up and preparation for the next cycle kick in immediately, as mappers analyze their analyses to see where they could have done better; vigilantly watch out for mapping tweaks that municipalities and taxing districts forget to tell them about; and produce fun-with-maps post-election summaries. Visiting St. Louis County election headquarters one afternoon, I noticed a change in décor: The board room and several other usually blank walls were festooned with large new maps plotting which kind of voting machine people preferred in the 2018 midterm elections. (In St. Louis County, in 2018 and 2019, you could still choose paper or plastic at the supermarket, and touchscreen or paper ballot at the voting booth.) The map was not downtime busy work. Early in 2019, the county launched a search for an entirely new voting system, and voters' preferences for paper ballots—mostly on security grounds—would eventually prove a deciding factor in the purchase.

When they took their current jobs, the mapping guys could probably have anticipated some of the complexities of the work they were taking on. After all, they make maps for a living. They know how complicated maps can be. They've internalized the lessons learned from snafus. Surely, Ryan's Eagle Scout optimism, Hartnett's IT expertise, and McLaughlin's political acuity boosted their confidence in their ability to take on whatever hurdles might come. What they couldn't have known was that their job descriptions were about to expand exponentially.

5

Wranglers

India's April 2019 election, with over nine
hundred million eligible voters, required
approximately one million polling places.
Eleven million government workers traveled
by foot, road, train, helicopter, boat, camel,
and elephant to get the job done.

—Reuters, May 22, 2019

IN NOVEMBER 2018, DEPENDING on where you lived in the
US at the time, you might have voted at the Su Nueva Laundromat in Chicago, the Columbarium & Funeral Home in San
Francisco, Theisen's Home & Auto Store in Dubuque, Iowa,
or the lifeguard station in Venice Beach, California. When it
comes to polling places, it's not all school gyms and church
social halls anymore.

These oddball choices can lead to some intriguing possibilities. You could combine voting with working on your seventen split at West County Lanes in Manchester, Missouri. You
might kick the tires of a new SUV while waiting in line to
vote at Napleton Northwestern Chrysler in Chicago. Or you
could perfect your backstroke in Los Angeles's Echo Deep Pool

and then mark your *X* next to your candidate of choice—but, please, don't drip on the voting machine or the ballots.

Certainly, the old standbys are still standing by: Taxpayer supported institutions, like schools or municipal buildings, are required by law, in most states, to be available for voting. But sometimes, polling-place spotters must get creative, especially in sparsely developed areas they've dubbed "polling-place deserts." So, when they can't find a building that satisfies our collective notion of a Norman Rockwell zone, they resort to places like the Fiesta Mart grocery store in Houston. Or, if there's no suitable edifice at all—as happened in 2018 in the Logan Park area of Chicago—people might find themselves in a U-Haul tricked out for voting, strategically parked on a neighborhood street. And if you are in a Chicago-area jail, you may discover that—depending on what you're accused or convicted of—there's a polling place near your cell.

Whether it is conventional or out of the ordinary, your polling place is ground zero for democracy on election days. But, as with many other aspects of voting, it's easy to take polling places for granted. If all goes as expected, they're open when we show up; they're set up and functioning; we get in and get out, without noticing much about where we've voted or why that location has been chosen. We get accustomed to voting at the same elementary school library, election in and election out, and we like it that way. It's simple: Here's where we live, and here's where we vote. Case closed. Well, not exactly. Procuring polling places, setting them up for elections, and making sure they are safe and secure is considerably more complicated than voters typically assume.

"What people don't realize is that there's a lot of logistics and planning, and it's not just one day the magic fairies have arrived and everything's ready. There's a lot going on," said St. Louis County's deputy director Christian Tolbert, who often heads out to polling places on troubleshooting missions on big election days.

For the 2018 midterms, there were about 230,000 polling places to wrangle in the United States, making polling-place management a critical but largely unacknowledged job. Somebody in every one of the country's 8,000 election jurisdictions draws the assignment of identifying, assigning, and managing polling places. As straws go, it might not be the shortest, but the job is fraught with complications, such as the risk of public confusion or anger when a polling place is moved.

Managing polling places can be a relatively low-anxiety job in a small jurisdiction where everyone votes, say, at the village hall. It's much more complicated in places like New York City, with upwards of 1,200 polling locations, and Philadelphia, with 829.

With those factors in mind, I was surprised when the mapping guys in St. Louis County informed me in a casual, oh-by-the-way remark, that in their office, they are the polling-place guys, too. It seems like a big ask, when you take into account the burden they shoulder in keeping their jumble of a jurisdiction under control geographically. But they managed to convince me—and themselves, I suspect—that there are logical reasons to marry up the two areas of responsibility.

The merger took place in 2018, as the result of an unhappy circumstance. Their predecessor, Dan Sigler, was renowned for his encyclopedic knowledge and institutional memory of the county's polling sites and their idiosyncrasies. "He could pull out a list of four hundred polling places, pick out one and say, 'Oh, this church location. The pastor retired and they're closing down the congregation. We're going to have to find someplace else.' That's how detailed his knowledge was. He would just know the internal processes of these organizations that we had no idea existed. The depth and the breadth of his knowledge was quite magnificent," said Ryan.

Sadly, Sigler died in 2018. His absence left a gaping hole in expertise that would be tough to patch. With the symbiosis between mapping, precincts, and polling places, and with the recent addition of advanced technology, fusing the two functions made sense; and the mapping guys added polling-place management to their to-do lists.

They took on a big task. Job one, after making sure that maps are accurate, is to make sure that every precinct has a polling place. "That was one of the easier jobs because many of the existing polling locations have been used for years. It's a history thing. We didn't have to start from scratch," said Ryan.

Sometimes, though, they do, and that entails some detailed research. A basic description of what they're looking for are big rooms in buildings with enough parking to accommodate the expected turnout of voters. But, of course, it's not that simple. While some criteria are obvious, such as proximity to voters served by the location and permission of the property owners, others can be vexing.

The federal Election Assistance Commission devotes quite a bit of space on its website to polling-place evaluation, a task that means looking at entrances and exits, measuring hallways, observing traffic flow in the parking lot, sketching out how the room could be set up for voting, visualizing where voters would stand in line, and making sure the location will accommodate disabled voters. Among the recommended tools for an initial site visit are a fifteen-foot tape measure and a bubble level to assess slopes in parking lots and on walkways.

But even after a site has been approved, and the people who run it agree to open the doors before their first cup of coffee, and then keep it open perhaps until bedtime, election staff must follow up with double- and triple-checking. That's a top priority before every election. Even managers of longstanding locations can drop out or forget that there's an election, especially in odd-numbered years. "We contact every location before every election, to make sure they're still in," said Bill Hartnett, who devised a checklist called Survey 123 that goes out far in advance to the contact at every polling place, to determine availability.

"But closer to the election, when we check in again, there's always someone—sometimes a person who said 'yes' on the survey a couple of months earlier—who says, 'Huh? There's an election on April 5? I totally forgot, and, by the way, we're remodeling that whole area, so we won't be able to accommodate you this time.' That's when we start to scramble," said Ryan.

That's exactly what happened when the prestigious PGA national golf championship came to St. Louis in 2018. Tournament week coincided with the August 7 primary election, and unbeknownst to the polling-place wranglers, the PGA had leased every school parking lot in a several-mile radius from the tournament site for the entire week, pre-empting six polling places. Ryan and his team found out about that move two months before the election and started scoping out nearby churches as alternative sites. "But, fun story," said Ryan, "the PGA had bought up all the church parking lots, too."

That's when the high-tech GIS mapping system came to the rescue. Ryan called up information from GIS—mapping layers, parcels of land and aerial imagery—to visualize the location of the big buildings in the affected area. The next step is an example of the need for polling-place managers to have public-relations skills: "I just made a list, and I started phoning and saying, 'Hello, can you help us out?'"

Some polling-place problems are self-inflicted, throwing managers unaccustomed to high visibility—or any visibility at all—into the spotlight. Six weeks before the November 2018 election, the county clerk in Dodge City, Kansas, announced that she was relocating the city's lone polling place. The reason for the move, she explained, was upcoming construction at the city center where voting normally took place. Voters are notoriously touchy about moving to new polling places, but this development transcended mere personal preferences: The new location was outside the city limits, separated from the city by train tracks, and a mile from the nearest bus stop. Minority and low-income voters called the move racially and economically discriminatory. The ACLU filed a lawsuit. National news media came to town. The county clerk, besieged, spent the days and weeks before the election defending the move, which voting rights activists continue to cite as an example of deliberate disenfranchisement or, at least, a flagrant disregard for voters' needs.

Not everyone takes that view, however. Eric Fey, whose sympathies understandably lie with innocent, under-fire election administrators, cautioned against jumping to conclusions about nefarious motives in moving or closing polling places. He offered an Occam's Razor explanation. "In many cases, it's simple economic necessity," he told me. "And in others, it's just a matter of a very busy county clerk, with lots of other responsibilities besides elections, just trying to make their job a little easier for themselves by reducing the number of polling places that have to be managed."

That is not to say that intentional polling-place shenanigans don't occur. News reports of long waits at polling places, especially in low-income and minority neighborhoods, are a regular feature of big elections across the country. The evidence generally is anecdotal, and it can be tempting to dismiss it. But a recent, more scientifically based study appeared to confirm what many minority voters have complained about for years.

"Using data from millions of smartphone users, we quantify a racial disparity in voting wait times across a nationwide sample of polling places during the 2016 US presidential election," reported M. Keith Chen, of Cornell University, in 2019. "Relative to entirely-white neighborhoods, residents of entirely-black neighborhoods waited 29 percent longer to vote and were 74 percent more likely to spend more than thirty minutes at their polling place."

The researchers don't speculate on the reasons behind these disparities—and there could be legitimate, contributing circumstances—but it stands to reason that a mal-intentioned polling-place manager could influence an election by jiggering locations to make it less convenient to vote in targeted demographic areas. So, administrators committed to equal access must be on the lookout for these kinds of inequities—whatever the cause.

▪

A uniquely twenty-first century complication is that schools—the locations most frequently associated in the public mind with voting—are increasingly reluctant about participating.

"Unfortunately, with all the school shootings we've seen in recent years, schools are wary of letting strangers in," said Ryan. "We need to negotiate more now with school administrators because they need to deal with parents calling in worried about the safety of their kids on election day. As far as I'm aware, there's never been a voter-related incident in a school. But with everything that happens in the news, there are a lot of people who are very fearful about that potentiality. It's an understandable security issue." Case in point: Late in 2019, North Dakota's Rapid City School District notified the county clerk that they were pulling all their schools from polling-place duty, precisely because of safety issues raised by parents.

It's rare for an organization to proactively ask to be a polling site. Taxpayer-supported buildings may be obliged to act as polling places if requested, but some jurisdictions are moving away from even asking. Nationwide, 90 percent of polling places are in schools and churches. But many of them have changed the rules of engagement. Some school districts have declared election day a school holiday, as a way of reducing the perceived risk to students. Others have pushed voting to sectioned-off portions of their buildings, designating a separate entrance for voters and putting the voting facility in a space where voters and students won't cross paths.

In a recent election, one St. Louis County school adopted that strategy. But when Rob Ryan showed up to check out the new configuration, he noticed a curious adaptation. The school had used gardening mulch to create a separate path to the new voting entrance. "There are requirements for disabled accessibility, and I questioned whether the mulch path met the criteria set out by the Americans with Disabilities Act," said

Ryan. "That's when the building manager, with a straight face, declared that there was no problem. He was using, he claimed, 'ADA-approved mulch.'"

The job of polling-place jockey requires a lot of advance work: identifying locations, signing contracts, coordinating with custodial workers, figuring out parking, arranging for keys, coordinating with local law enforcement, and working out the kinks that make each location unique. Polling-site planners are in the public-relations business as well, because they need to develop good rapport with facilities managers and custodial staff, whose cooperation is critical. "I'm constantly amazed that people are willing to meet our poll workers at 5 a.m. on election day to make sure that the building gets open, the heat's on, and the chairs and tables are set up in time," said Ryan.

When there aren't enough suitable public buildings, or if they're not available for legitimate reasons, private facilities—including churches—enter the mix. About half of St. Louis County's four hundred polling places are in private facilities. There is a cost to that—a rental fee. Not a big cost, but an expense, nonetheless, and one that is apparently not well understood. At a recent meeting of St. Louis County's board of elections, one commissioner brought up the subject. "Why," the commissioner asked, "does the election board pay to use a room at nearby Washington University, which is one of the richest colleges in the US, with a multibillion-dollar endowment?" "They're helping us out," explained one of the assistant directors, patiently. "They have expenses—assigning a worker to show up early, to set up tables for voting, and to stay as late as we need them to be there. We think it's worth the expense, which is all of a hundred and fifty bucks."

One way around some of these polling-site complexities is to move away from the traditional neighborhood precinct model and go to a "vote-center" system. In that model, election officials open a smaller number of strategically located voting sites for several days leading up to an election. Any qualified voter can vote at any vote center. In theory, vote centers are more convenient because people can vote near their workplaces or schools, for example, rather than having to race home to their neighborhood before polls close.

One jurisdiction that has gone all in for vote centers is Los Angeles County, the biggest jurisdiction in the country. "L.A. is radically altering the way we vote," proclaimed the *Los Angeles Times* in February 2020. "Get ready for big changes."

For the 2020 elections, the county is ditching its 4,400 neighborhood polling sites and replacing them with 1,000 vote centers. "There are no longer wrong places to vote in L.A. County," Dean Logan, who runs elections in the county, told the *Los Angeles Times*. "Every voting location is the right place to vote."

Although St. Louis County has no plans to make a similar switch, it's probably reassuring for mapping guys everywhere to know that morphing to the new model doesn't eliminate the need for their skills. It just changes the focus of the wrangling, placing increased emphasis on demographics. Mapping played a big role in educating the public about the change. L.A. County published detailed "story maps" to visualize proposed vote center locations, taking into consideration factors that voters care about, such as the centers' proximity to geographically isolated populations; low-income communities; voters with disabilities; language-minority communities; and public transportation. They even computed estimated point-to-point drive times, a significant factor in traffic-clogged Los Angeles.

Currently, sixteen states allow jurisdictions to use vote centers on election day, according to the National Conference of State Legislatures: Arizona, Arkansas, California, Colorado, Hawaii, Indiana, Iowa (for some elections), Kansas, Nevada, New Mexico, North Dakota, South Dakota, Tennessee, Texas, Utah, and Wyoming.

▪

But whether they're setting up neighborhood polling places or vote centers, even the most obsessive planners can get blindsided on election day. In Chandler, Arizona, poll workers arrived at sunrise at their site, the Golf Academy of America, to discover that, overnight, a bank had foreclosed on the business. It was padlocked, with all the election supplies inside, including ballots. The county recorder, charged with running elections, scrambled to find a new location and arranged for delivery of replacement equipment. Workers set it up outside, transforming the parking lot into a pop-up polling place.

There are many such potential potholes and detours. On a primary day in Totowa, New Jersey, a car driven by a poll worker crashed into the fire station that was being used as a polling place. In 2019, there were also reports of out-of-control cars accidentally slamming into polling sites in Mississippi, Connecticut, and Texas. One observer has suggested, perhaps tongue-in-cheek, that in searching for potential polling sites, election managers might try to avoid locations with large plate-glass windows.

Less headline worthy, but more typical, are problems with one of the most mundane bits of polling-place equipment—keys. Often, administrators mail them out or deliver them in advance to trusted election workers—so that custodial workers don't have to arrive at 5 a.m. It's impossible to know how many election days start with keys that don't fit, that jam in locks, or that otherwise highly responsible polling-place supervisors simply leave at home in the 4 a.m. rush to get to work on time. And it doesn't take much to disrupt the schedule. At a small city hall polling place in St. Louis County, workers couldn't open the doors until 5:30 a.m. because the mayor, who was bringing the key, had a flat tire. Or this: "I've had to send technicians to polling sites to help get the door open because when the key didn't seem to fit the lock, nobody thought to try turning it over to see if it worked that way," said Christian Tolbert.

"You pretty much know how the day is going to be by 6 a.m., because the calls from workers wrestling with polling-place issues come in early," said Eric Fey, who has, in his tenure as director of elections, dispatched himself to a polling place or two in the early morning hours to apply a hip check to a stuck door, or even break a window to gain access.

Getting all the polls open at the same time is a critical aspect of ensuring election fairness, and voters notice when polling places are late in opening. Studies consistently show that poll-opening time is a peak period for voting, with as many as 15 percent of voters arriving first thing in the morning. So, it's a moment of high visibility for election operations. When the line doesn't start moving at the designated time, it's obvious to voters, and they can be quick to lodge complaints with election-rights advocates or to notify the media. "On any given election day, we'll get a call from some reporter asking where the longest lines are, so that they can race out there and try to drum up a scandal story," said Fey. "They don't ever seem to ask us to tell them where things are operating most efficiently."

So Fey, Stream, and their counterparts across the US are on high alert in the early morning hours of election day. They're tracking polling places, and they don't breathe easily until they're all up and running. Starting the voting at the same time everywhere is a measure of fairness and equal access. It's also a leading indicator, in public opinion, of how well you're doing your job.

Getting past the opening bell is critical, but polling-place managers don't go off duty at 7 a.m. Closing time is critical, as well, especially in high-stakes elections, when some after-work voters show up at the very last minute. In one election, Fey took a call from a local television station, whose reporter said, "I have it on good authority that one of your polling places was already closed at 5:15 this afternoon. They're supposed to be open until 7 o'clock. How do you explain that?"

"He was correct," said Fey, "but only because that polling location had never been open that day, as that area of the county was not part of the special election."

As carefully as they might evaluate the suitability of polling locations, and as closely as they try to stay in contact with facilities staff at polling sites, election managers sometimes learn, too late, that things are not always as advertised. In a report filed at the end of the day in an April election, one poll worker complained about arrangements at the fire station serving as their polling place: "We have been relegated to the truck bays in the rear of this building for at least three elections," the poll worker wrote. "There's no air conditioning back there, but up until now, they've let us work inside. Today, we're stuck in the bays because they don't want us to mess up their new carpeting."

Sometimes, problems come out of nowhere. During one election in St. Louis County, when hardly anything else went wrong, Bill Hartnett fielded a mid-morning report about a heavy-duty chain stretched—and padlocked—between concrete stanchions on either side of the road in front of a polling place. After Hartnett called two police departments, who said, "Not our jurisdiction," Fey stepped in, called the chief of a nearby fire department, and convinced him to send out a crew to cut the chain. "Another problem solved," commented Fey wryly, adding it to his list of unpredictable election-day quirks, large and small.

Not long after that election day, the mapping guys-slash-wranglers found out that their jobs were about to get yet more complicated. The department was on a quest to buy an entirely new voting system. When the decision came down just weeks later, the wranglers had a whole new mission that would mean reevaluating every polling place in the district.

6

The Big Shop

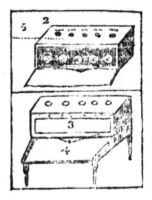

Using an early voting machine, circa 1838, voters in London, England dropped a brass ball into a hole in a wooden box. The hole was labeled with the candidate's name. The "ballot" advanced a clockwork counter one step, before falling into a tray on the front of the device, in clear view of the election judges.

–Douglas W. Jones, A Brief Illustrated History of Voting, *2001*

YOU DON'T USUALLY HEAR a cheer break out in the small conference room where the big-dog election commissioners meet. So, in early September 2019, when office workers at St. Louis County election headquarters heard "woo-hoo's" emanating from room 110, they knew something was up. In an uncharacteristically raucous moment in that more typically staid setting, voting-rights activists shared high fives, applauded and even hugged each other when the St. Louis County Board of Elections voted unanimously to purchase a desperately needed new voting system that would bring up-to-date security and technology to voters in the jurisdiction.

The activists had come to the meeting to make their last-ditch appeal for voting machines that would use paper ballots. Seated on mismatched, past-their-prime swivel chairs, some of the people crammed into the small conference room had been pushing for a reliably unhackable voting system for more than ten years. So, the vote was, indeed, a big deal, and about time, they said.

"We finally got what we wanted," said Cynthia Richards, who, as co-director of Missourians for Transparent and Secure Elections, had led the charge. Richards had become a familiar and outspoken presence in Missouri's state capitol and in election circles, testifying on behalf of statewide voting-reform legislation and persistently pursuing decision-makers with phone calls, emails, and in-person visits. The vote in St. Louis County was a major victory and a big get because, as the largest election jurisdiction in the state, St. Louis County could set the standard. "They did the right thing," she said.

But, as hard-won as it seemed for voting-rights advocates, the baseline decision to buy a new voting system for the county was the easy part for the board and staff. Choosing among the options for a new system was a much tougher challenge.

Ask anyone in the election office about the aging system in use since 2006, and the eye-rolling commenced. Everybody, from top managers to poll workers, could tell stories about the many ways that the department's thirteen-year-old voting machines could and did go wrong—with increasing frequency in recent years.

Voters had been complaining, too. A Republican committeewoman I met during a meeting proclaimed, with absolute certainty, that when she voted in 2016, she pressed the button for Donald Trump on her touchscreen machine, but it showed that she had voted for Hillary Clinton. She tried it three times, but it continued to happen, she insisted. I initially doubted her story, chalking it up to conspiracy-theory propaganda. But I was wrong. It was quite possible, Eric Fey told me in a subsequent conversation, because the old machines tended to go out of calibration.

"It didn't actually register the vote for the wrong candidate, but you could press a button over here on the lower left side of your screen, and it might appear to be placing your vote on the upper right side, next to the wrong candidate," he explained. "It's like being out of alignment, and it happened quite a bit as the machines aged."

Like too many voting systems in other jurisdictions around the country, St. Louis County's was not only technologically way behind the curve, but also mechanically broken beyond repair. They needed everything: new computers, new voting machines, new software, new scanners, a new tabulating system, new cables and connectors, and a new security system.

Even the way they deployed equipment to polling places needed a rethink. Lined up in neat rows in the department's warehouse were the county's four hundred, grayish-green transport cases—banged-up metal boxes one might describe as man-sized safes. They looked like they'd been around since World War II. They served as symbols of how overdue for change the county was. And with the 2020 presidential election approaching like a freight train, change was becoming an emergency.

"If we had to go into the next cycle with what we had, it would have been dicey, to say the least," said Rick Stream, facing a packed, high-stakes election calendar in 2020. There would be a lot of opportunities to get it right—or wrong. The equipment was simply too risky to deploy in such an important year.

"We weren't looking forward to 2020," said Fey. "I'm not sure anyone in election administration is." Statistics bear him out. In a 2018 study by the Brennan Center for Justice, researchers learned that a wide swath of election jurisdictions were desperate for new equipment. More than 120 election officials in thirty-one states said they needed to upgrade their voting machines before 2020, but only about a third of them said they had enough money for the project. Forty states were using machines that were at least a decade old, and forty-five reported using equipment that's not even manufactured anymore.

"We are driving the same car in 2019 that we were driving in 2004, and the maintenance costs are mounting up," one South Carolina election official told the Brennan Center's researchers. He said that he felt lucky to be able to find any spare parts at all.

Even though election managers call the situation an emergency, states and counties have been notoriously stingy with funding. In some cases, new election equipment has been seen as a frill, not a priority. As Wendy Noren, formerly the legislative co-chair of the Missouri County Clerks Association, once bitterly observed, "I've got county commissioners that don't mind spending a million dollars on a road that will serve a thousand people. But the thought of needing a million dollars for election equipment that will serve sixty thousand people is just beyond comprehension to them."

■

St. Louis County had been using touchscreen machines—known as DREs, or direct-recording electronic voting machines—purchased in 2006 from election-equipment giant ES&S for ten million dollars. The old DREs used technology now viewed as outdated, possibly tamper-prone, and not adequately verifiable. The whole system operated on the now-antique Windows XP system, which in its day was considered highly secure, but which had not been updated or even supported in years. The county's 1,800 DREs were a constant source of frustration for poll workers and voters: The paper rolls that tracked votes developed an expletive-engendering tendency to jam. Some screens were so scratched that they obscured portions of the ballot. Some of the machines simply refused to boot up.

They were at the point of no return. "We couldn't even fill in incrementally with more recent models, because they didn't work with Windows XP," Fey explained.

To keep things running as the machines aged, Fey and his crew had been improvising madly. A few years earlier, Fey learned that the election office in Troy, Missouri, about one hundred miles away, had experienced an equipment disaster, when the roof of their warehouse caved in during a rainstorm, soaking all of their DREs—which, coincidentally, were identical to those used in St. Louis County. Troy's insurance policy covered the purchase of new equipment, so they were getting ready to junk what they had. Fey saw an opportunity and grabbed the salvageable machines to cannibalize them for spare parts.

"The dirty secret was that somebody else's crisis was our good luck," said Fey. But he and his team knew that they couldn't continue to count on *schadenfreude* moments like that to solve their problems. So, St. Louis County went shopping, with a budget of ten million dollars, but a bank account of just four million. Deciding which new system to spend millions of taxpayer dollars on was a tricky, time-consuming, and contentious process.

Of course, responsible election administrators don't just pick up the phone and order takeout for a ten-million-dollar purchase that is expected to last for ten years. The first step for Fey and his staff was to create a shopping list. That meant scores of hours of research, multiple meetings with local lawmakers and financial advisers, consultations with lawyers and election gurus, and keyboard time—lots of keyboard time—yielding a fifty-seven-page request for proposal (RFP).

This was their shot. They had to get it right. So, the RFP laid out every requirement that Fey and others could think of. It included—like those in most industries—pages of dense, boilerplate language that only a lawyer could love. Many of the specifications were commonsense, tried-and-true criteria that might seem obvious, but that in too many instances in the past had been overlooked, omitted, or ignored, causing election results to be clouded by doubt and viewed as untrustworthy or inaccurate. That's exactly what happened in the 2000 presidential election, when the punch-card system in Florida produced the infamous hanging and pregnant chads, creating havoc and triggering a Supreme Court challenge to the results.

"Until the 2000 election, in a lot of places, the local election office tended to be a sleepy, backwater operation," said Fey. "You just bumped along. Everything changed after 2000." And much of what happened still factors significantly into an election jurisdiction's equipment-buying decision.

America woke up after the uber-controversial 2000 election, and in 2002 Congress passed the Help America Vote

Act (HAVA). The act marked the first time in US history that the federal government had funded an election reform effort. HAVA initially allocated $3.3 billion to states for updating their voting equipment. Election administrators all over the country—including St. Louis County—gobbled up the funds, which is how St. Louis County upgraded, in 2006, from punch-card voting to the DREs they were finally ditching thirteen years later.

HAVA also created the US Election Assistance Commission (EAC), which continues to plug away today. EAC is an independent, bipartisan national organization. Its carefully wrought guidelines for voting systems have achieved gospel status among election officials everywhere. EAC also issues certifications—but not recommendations—for commercially produced voting machines and systems, a function that would play an important role for Fey and his evaluation committee when vendors would later come to call.

Clearly, the RFP's writing team had studied EAC's "Voluntary Voting System Guidelines" carefully because they formed the baseline for the proposal.

Note the word "voluntary." In America's federal system, we don't have a centralized voting authority—other than something called the US Constitution, of course. But that foundational document deals only with principles, not specifics. Voting rules are up to the states, and states have differing ideas about what constitutes a fair voting system. The Voting Rights Act of 1965 was a noble attempt to smooth out the differences and ensure equality, but even that didn't stick: The US Supreme Court essentially gutted the Voting Rights Act in the 2013 *Shelby County v. Holder* case. The court ruled, by a 5–4 vote, that the law was unconstitutional because it was based on forty-year-old data, making it "no longer responsive to current needs."

Worse yet—or perhaps better, if you're a fan of decentralization—is the patchwork of voting structures within states. While some have statewide rules and criteria, others—Missouri among them—leave decisions about equipment and procedures up to individual counties or townships. Under this non-system, voting is essentially an unregulated free-for-all, in which for-profit corporations, who design and sell the equipment we vote on, flex considerable muscle.

So, EAC's standards, even in their voluntary state of being, offer at least a baseline for continuity and uniformity. Admittedly, though, reading through the EAC's list of fifteen principles and guidelines, it's tempting to glaze over and skip a sentence or a section here and there. But doing that would miss the point. Sometimes, I told myself when I found my attention wandering, you need to remind yourself of the bottom-line basics that we tend to take for granted. As a few examples, EAC's guidelines remind voting authorities that their systems need to work not just in controlled demonstrations, but also in real-world conditions, where power goes out, people drip sweat on ballots, and voters forget to bring their reading glasses. Also, the public should be able to understand and verify the operations of the voting system throughout the election, says EAC. An error in system software or hardware shouldn't cause an undetectable change in election results. And there needs to be a reliable system for checking whether the outcome is correct.

With those and other basic principles as its underpinnings, St. Louis County's RFP went on to specify a wide range of requirements that even the most engaged voter probably never thinks of. The details were in a six-page section, with eighty-one numbered bullet points.

This is the heart of the wonky part. But it's worth a close reading because it provides a sense of the things that keep election administrators awake at night. It was as much a worry list as it was a set of demands. One can almost visualize more than one person bursting into Fey's office and leaning over his shoulder to make sure that he had included a provision for that one thing that nearly wrecked an election day—or their job.

Fey's RFP was fairly typical of others floating around in 2019, he told me. But no two election jurisdictions are the same. And sometimes, what sets one jurisdiction's voting-system requirements apart from others is how it reflects specific problems that election managers have faced in the past.

There's much evidence of that fighting-the-last-war approach in the St. Louis County RFP. You would probably have to be a true election junkie to notice, but it's in there. For example, the RFP requires that a new system be able to "easily add or subtract candidates and/or issues as a result of late court rulings." You can draw a straight line between that requirement and a last-minute court ruling in November 2018 that forced Fey to remove a smoking-ban issue from the ballot. That ruling sent Fey's tech staff scrambling. "We were reprogramming our system until the very last minute," he recalled. He would rather not have to do that again. But if he does, he wants it to be a much easier fix.

Another bullet point in the RFP called for the ability to "manipulate font type and all ballot text and images during layout … without requiring the use of any external devices or processes." It sounds picayune, but it circles right back to another 2018 near debacle, when the Missouri statewide ballot was the longest in state history. There were too many contests and not enough room on the 8.5" x 19" maximum ballot size that the county's old optical scanners could handle. To make it work, Fey had to negotiate edits, within legal limits, with sponsoring groups and the Missouri secretary of state, and then redesign the ballot with a smaller—much smaller—font size. Those changes, of course, made it harder for voters to read.

"As you can probably imagine, there were a lot of complaints about that," said Fey. With that situation still gnawing at him, Fey included the ballot-design provision in the RFP.

St. Louis County's quirky election structure—with its maze of school districts, taxing districts, fire districts, water districts, state rep districts, senatorial districts, and others—adds yet another layer of requirements for voting equipment vendors. To make sure that voters are getting the right options, the election board must generate hundreds of customized ballots, known in the election lexicon as "ballot styles."

Just to be clear, the term "ballot style" does not refer to a color, a shape, a size, or a layout. A ballot style displays the unique combination of contests and candidates that voters see on a screen or on a paper ballot, depending on where they live within the St. Louis County matrix. In the April 2019 municipal elections, for example, St. Louis County had to generate three hundred different ballot styles. As a result, the RFP said that, if you're going to play in St. Louis County, you must accommodate this custom-ballot idiosyncrasy. And that is not a normal task for some voting machine makers. In fact, one vendor let Fey know that it was not replying to the RFP because the company couldn't produce the necessary variety of ballot styles.

Here's another special consideration: The last time St. Louis County got new voting equipment, it compromised on a hybrid system of touchscreen voting (DREs) and preprinted, hand-marked paper ballots recorded by optical scanners. The touchscreen option caught on quickly with voters, who viewed it as more high tech, thus presumably more accurate. A local survey revealed that, during the forty most recent elections (over about ten years), 70 to 80 percent of voters chose what they perceived to be the more convenient touchscreen technology. In presidential elections, it was more of a fifty–fifty split. But a determined and vocal paper-ballot minority still preferred the fill-in-the-oval, lower-tech option. (Ironically, these often-maligned, so-called Luddites, were prescient, as EAC's more recent standard for voting verifiability is the old-fashioned paper ballot, or at least a paper trail.)

But hand-marked ballots can be problematic, too. Vote counters have seen it all. Many people over- or undershoot the oval. They insert *X*s or check marks in ovals designed to be filled in, standardized-test style. Some don't turn their paper ballots over to side two; some write on the blank second side of the ballot. Others mark more than one candidate and try to cross out their errors. And then there was the voter who, given the option to vote "Yes" or "No" on a local proposition, indicated his choice by coloring in the "o" of "No."

In his department's "2016 Biennial Report to the Public," Fey included photos of several of the most idiosyncratically marked ballots in that election cycle. One looks like a pirate's treasure map, with *X*s where ink ovals should have been and a large arrow drawn across the page. Presumably, it meant something to the voter, but neither a scanning machine nor a human eye could decipher the voter's intent. The election-day remedy to these issues is for voters to report their errors to election officials on the spot and to then "spoil" the messed-up ballot and replace it with another. But apparently, some voters either don't know that this procedure exists, are in a hurry, or just don't want to admit that they goofed.

Anticipating these kinds of problems, knowing that many St. Louis County voters were going to insist on hand-marked ballots, and not prepared to hire psychics to interpret voters' intentions, Fey included these specifications in the RFP:

> 60: The voting system … must possess the capability of processing a ballot with a blank second or back page if no election data flows to the second or back page.
>
> 64: The system … must possess the capability to distinguish common acceptable marks in addition to the prescribed marks on a ballot (i.e., a commonly accepted "X" in place of the prescribed, fully shaded oval).

There probably is no system that can decipher all the variations of cross-outs, overwrites, squiggly lines, and scrawled notes that pose as votes on some hand-marked ballots. But the RFP asked vendors to at least try.

Other parts of the RFP laid out requirements for recording votes, tabulating results, and ensuring security. It even gets down to nitty-gritty bits like the need for a backup battery system that would work for four hours in case of a power outage, and the requirement that equipment not be too heavy for poll workers to heft and break down at the end of the day. It was an exhaustive list—probably exhausting to write, and definitely exhausting to wade through—but it had to be. Missing an element could be disastrous.

The decision would be momentous, said Rick Stream. Launching a search for a multimillon-dollar system was as big and daunting a challenge as any election administrator could take on, perhaps in an entire career. "We were deciding on something that would affect our operations for the next decade. It would touch every department. It became our highest priority because people need to have full confidence that their votes mean something. We knew we had to be very deliberative."

That approach, it should be noted, does not match the process some other jurisdictions used when buying new voting systems in 2019. Many—too many, if you follow election news—went single source: They just called up their existing vendor and bought new machines, forking over hundreds of thousands, if not millions, of dollars without any attempt at comparison shopping. Some bought from the vendor whose lobbyists spent the most in their districts. Voters, legislators, and voting-rights activists called some of those decisions into question when the new equipment rolled out and didn't perform as advertised, as happened in several Pennsylvania counties in late 2019.

A worrying number of other jurisdictions were still dithering as the calendar rolled over to 2020. In early January, some counties in Georgia and Tennessee had yet to allocate funds for new voting equipment to replace their vintage-2001 machinery. It was going to be a mad scramble to decide on a vendor, take delivery, and get poll workers up to speed in time for presidential primary elections.

▪

St. Louis County's equipment quest had a routine beginning but a surprise ending. Early in 2019, Fey and his team pushed their RFP out to the major players in the voting-system world. Prospective suppliers had until March to submit questions, send in their proposals, and try to convince a panel of picky evaluators that they had the right stuff at the right price. All Fey, Stream, and the rest of the team could do at that point was to cross their fingers and hope that something workable and affordable would boomerang back to them.

The universe of voting machine vendors is small. It's a dog-eat-dog business, with a long and complicated history of mergers, buyouts, rebranding, bankruptcies, controversies over marketing strategies, and reports of conflicts of interest with political decision makers and foreign oligarchs. As of 2019, the EAC listed just eighteen registered manufacturers in the US, but prominently cautioned that registration does not constitute endorsement. Many vendors offer a smorgasbord of systems with varying capabilities—of which some are certified under EAC's standards, while others are still in the testing phase.

EAC's standards, remember, are voluntary. Other than EAC's nonbinding criteria, there's hardly any oversight at the federal, state, or local level of quality control or standards for purchasing voting equipment. So, while many jurisdictions—including St. Louis County—use EAC certification and standards as baseline requirements, they're essentially out there on their own buying expensive systems expected to meet voters' needs and ensure fair, trustworthy elections over many election cycles.

Of the eighteen EAC registered companies, three dominate the US market: The largest is ES&S, which reportedly controls about fifty percent of the country's election-system market. Dominion and Hart InterCivic share most of the rest. They're under pressure, too. Big voting-equipment replacements come along only occasionally, and the federal funding that many states rely on is limited. Of the $3.6 billion appropriated by HAVA—which includes a supplementary $380 million added in 2018—states had burned through roughly 85 percent by the end of 2018, according to the National Conference of State Legislatures. The pot of money is drying up, and Congress has shown little inclination to pass additional election-reform legislation that could replenish it. So, there's a lot riding on every sale. And vendors can pass that pressure on to jurisdictions pushing the shopping cart.

"There's a narrow set of vendors. They all know we need stuff," said Fey, shortly after the RFP went out. "And once you buy a voting system, you are stuck with it for a long time. They have to make their money when they can because we are making purchases only once in a while. But we don't want to be over a barrel."

Four preliminary inquiries came in. An initial review winnowed the field to three. They turned out to be, no surprise, the usual suspects: ES&S, Dominion, and Hart InterCivic, all of whom the department then invited to submit full proposals. An eight-person evaluation team, drawn from several departments, lugged around the applicants' thick binders of technical specifications, sales pitches, and cost quotations and buried themselves in the details for weeks. Deputy directors Julie Leicht and Christian Tolbert rode herd. Fey, Stream, and the commissioners were recused from the evaluation process, to take any potential personal bias out of the equation.

Being selected to serve on the evaluation team could be viewed as either an honor or a punishment. "It's a lot of extra work," said Rick Stream. "They were paid for the additional hours, but I like to think that the job was more than just the hours. To be in on this huge decision is, I think, a big deal and sort of a privilege." Stream also noted that to keep the process fair and unbiased, "as soon as we set up the committee, we shut down all communications between vendors and any of us here in the office—not just the evaluation team, but all of us."

The team used an elaborate scoring system to rate dozens of criteria, from the all-important security concerns to ease-of-use and transportability. Cost was, of course, a factor, but the RFP made it clear that the lowest-cost bidder would not necessarily win.

Ironically, the first shock was the sticker price. Low cost was not going to be a factor. "We were thinking ten million dollars," recalled Leicht, a veteran of several governmental departments before this one, and a committed professional who exudes efficiency and management savvy. She knew her way around RFPs, but this was her biggest. "They came in at more like thirteen million. That gave us pause, to say the least. Our equipment fund was already short six million dollars from our original estimate."

But, despite not knowing how they would make up that gaping budget deficit, they plunged ahead, scheduling demonstrations of each prospective system for the public and for department workers. The demos, live-streamed simultaneously on the department's Facebook page, drew full-house crowds. People who had worked as poll workers were eager to see how their jobs might change, get better or worse—or possibly be eliminated—with a new system. They asked a lot of questions, many of which reflected their frustration with the old DREs and their hope that a new system would be more reliable and easier to work with. At every session, someone asked about the weight of the equipment. There were many questions about paper, printers, toner, battery backup, and procedures for set-up and breakdown. These workers had been through it all, knew the old equipment's quirks inside out, and never wanted to unjam a paper roll again.

But even as they scrutinized the hands-on details, many were thinking about security as well. There were questions about bar codes, calibration, programming, internet connectivity, potential hacking, and accommodations for special-needs voters. One attendee wondered if the new equipment could be hijacked by a voter or poll worker to play the online game *Candy Crush*. To their credit, the salespeople—smooth operators clearly accustomed to these make-or-break situations—calmly fielded every question, even the many repeaters.

By the end of the decision-making cycle, the verdict seemed clear. A summary of evaluators' score sheets showed that Hart had come out on top.

Then, the plot twisted.

Because that's what the RFP asked for, all of the proposals had centered on ballot-marking systems, known as BMDs. They use touchscreen equipment to register voters' preferences onscreen, print the machine-marked paper ballot, and spit it out for the voter to review and then feed into a scanner. The ballot-marking devices do not count votes: They just mark them because, well, as the title says, they're ballot-marking devices, not ballot-counting devices. They are, as one sales rep described them, "nineteen-pound, vote-marking pens." And that was fine because BMDs had become all the rage for their ability to combine uniform ballot marking with the checkability of paper ballots.

Then—and here's the curveball—during one of Hart's meetings with the evaluation committee, a sales rep mentioned something called ballot-on-demand (BOD)—a configuration that prints one unmarked, plain-paper ballot at a time, customized to the voter at the check-in station. The voter takes the ballot to a table, fills in the ovals with a black pen and then runs it through in the scanner, which records the vote and sucks the ballot into the attached ballot box for safekeeping. The sales rep mentioned that option somewhat offhandedly, as a backup—for special-needs voters who might not be able to hand mark a ballot—to the main BMD system that Hart was pushing.

"Until that presentation, we didn't even know such a thing existed," said Fey. The department had some printers in a back room that could be used to churn out ballots in special situations, but the machines weighed two hundred pounds each, so they weren't a practical, district-wide solution. The existence of a fully portable, integrated ballot-printing system came as a surprise. "I remember hearing people say that it might actually be a better option. It opened up a whole new possibility. We sort of just stumbled into it," said Fey.

They reopened the bidding, asking for ballot-on-demand proposals. Two of the three companies made convincing pitches. The third was almost pathetically half-hearted because that vendor clearly did not have a workable BOD system and had built its entire world around ballot-marking devices.

"Looking at the demos and the specs, Hart seemed to have the only BOD system that was battle-tested and ready for prime-time," said Fey. Plus, the total cost for the equipment, licensing, support, and the many other features of a voting-system contract was $6.9 million—an impressive bargain compared to the original bids.

"The reason that we weren't familiar with the BOD concept at the get-go was, I think, that these companies downplay them," Fey added. "They would much rather sell us the bigger, more expensive system. So, vendors are not aggressive in selling these systems, because they're not as lucrative as the BMDs."

Behind closed doors, staff and commissioners had diverging opinions on BMDs versus BODs. It seems logical that some would favor BMDs as the tech-forward option with the advantage of uniform ballot marking and the transparency of voter intent. Others presumably would lean toward ballots-on-demand as a way of enabling voting without the intermediation of a machine that might—accidentally or intentionally—distort the outcome. Ballot-marking devices, after all, were proliferating and had a proven track record. BODs, a much less popular option at that point, could be viewed as risky—as they were by several attendees at demonstration sessions—because they rely on off-the-shelf printers, commercially purchased paper, and toner—components that have failed poll workers in the past. And poll workers have long memories. BODs have the advantage, though, of eliminating the threat of another ballot-shortage fiasco like the one in 2016—one that everybody in St. Louis County remembers, and nobody wants to relive.

Julie Leicht was among the initial ballot-on-demand doubters, she told me after the decision came down. "At first, I wasn't convinced," she said. "I was one of those that thought we might be taking a step backwards because the public was so used to voting on a touchscreen. How would they view this?"

The voting-rights activists had pushed hard for hand-marked paper ballots all along, but they had met with pushback. One faction had lobbied for the elimination of all forms of mechanical voting, favoring old-style paper ballots, printed in large quantities before elections. "The biggest objections came from, of all places, St. Louis County," said Cynthia Richards.

Richards's comment struck me as odd, knowing Fey's commitment to innovation. When I asked him about it, I sensed that he felt misunderstood. "There are a few things there to unpack," he told me. "First, the statewide legislation they were proposing would have outlawed the DREs that we had at the time. We had no funds to get new voting equipment back then, so we certainly couldn't be in favor of a system that would upend what we had in place. Also, I can't imagine a scenario where I would be in favor of preprinted paper ballots." He was alluding, of course, to the 2016 ballot-shortage crisis that had threatened his job. He was not going there again.

Hart's configuration offered the best of both worlds, it seemed: hand-marked, paper ballots-on-demand, right at the polling place, saving millions of taxpayers' dollars. The paper ballot advocates won, too, but only because the board seren-dipitously got that late-breaking glimpse of the BOD option and jumped on it. That accidental turn of events may also have landed St. Louis County in the middle of an emerging debate over the election-integrity merits of BMDs versus BODs. As of late 2019, ballot-marking devices were the purchase of choice in many states and local jurisdictions: Georgia, South Caro-lina, and Delaware chose new ballot-marking device systems for their entire states. Philadelphia and Pittsburgh were nearly on-board. People who track these things estimated that around the country by the end of 2019, jurisdictions would have bought 130,000 new BMDs.

But some advocates for hand-marked paper ballots predict that BMDs could fall out of favor—just as the DREs did when controversial elections threw machine-based voting into doubt. Although he wasn't privy to the deliberations of the evaluation committee, Fey said he was "pretty sure that several members of the committee were kind of looking around the corner, saw some of the objections to BMDs that were emerging around the country, and thought, 'You know what? Maybe it's best if we just avoid that.'"

In the end, they adopted the ballot-on-demand system. Fey told me that St. Louis County was probably, at the time of the purchase, the only US election jurisdiction of its size that would be using BODs as its primary method of voting. Some had purchased a limited number of BODs to use for special-needs voters. Undoubtedly, others would be watching to see how well BODs worked on such a large scale.

But there was a remaining problem: They were still several million dollars shy of the final cost. The state of Missouri had kicked in a grand total of $160,000 toward the purchase. The board would have to get financing to bridge the gap.

They were fortunate to have $4 million on hand. The Help America Vote Act (HAVA), passed by Congress in 2002, freed up election jurisdictions, for the first time, to charge for the use of voting equipment. When Fey took over as director of elections in 2015, he discovered that St. Louis County hadn't been using that funding mechanism, and he pushed the board to put it in play to establish a new-equipment piggy bank. Since then, the board annually establishes a user fee for each piece of equipment per election—for example, $175 per polling-place printer—adds up the total countywide equipment cost, and divvies it up among the municipalities and taxing districts participating in a given election, according to their share of total registered voters. Over time, the fees have added up, so that the county's equipment war chest reached the $4 million it had in 2019.

"Without that fund, we would have had zero," said Fey. "With the equipment-replacement fund in place, we hope not to get caught short next time. We're trying to accumulate funds at a pace that will give us about ten million dollars over the next ten years, when the next new-equipment go-round is likely to hit us."

■

With the votes cast—it was unanimous, as boards like to be in public—the decision made, and final financing negotiations under way, everyone could breathe easier, but not for long. Until they field-test the hardware and software in a real election, the jury will be out on whether they made the right decision. Like everyone else around the country who has taken a similar plunge, St. Louis County can only wait and see. "2020," observed Fey, "will be the proof in the pudding for all of us."

"There's a ton of work to do," said Leicht after the board meeting adjourned and the cheering subsided. You could almost sense the synapses firing in her project-manager brain: She was already contemplating the slew of adaptations, procedural changes, training sessions, and public-education campaigns that the new system would necessitate. With a knowing wink, she added, "Now, the real fun begins."

7

Brawn and Brains

Less than two months before voting began in an election for governor, a fire in the Harris County, Texas election warehouse destroyed ten thousand pieces of electronic voting equipment valued at $30 million. The county had to start from scratch to rebuild its elections infrastructure and replace its $10 million warehouse.

–Houston Chronicle, *August 27, 2010*

WHILE TOP DECISION-MAKERS WERE still wrestling with which equipment to buy, Joe Winter, Craig Hite, and the warehouse crew they supervise were already on fast-forward. No matter what, the old system was a goner. The time had come to move on from the out-of-whack and out-of-favor machinery the warehouse crew had been MacGyvering election cycle after election cycle for more than a decade. Years earlier, the warehouse staff had taken maintenance in-house, becoming certified technicians, reducing costs, and ensuring the security of the equipment by never letting it out of their custody. Now, the job was to get rid of the clunky DREs, the outmoded optical scanners, and the battered metal transport cases—all of which combined to take up most of the territory in their work area.

Winter is brawny and somewhat grizzled, in a good-guy kind of way. Before joining the elections crew, he worked as a trucker, loading food and supplies onto airplanes. If you're going on a road trip, and you need to figure out how to fit twenty cubic feet of gear into the fourteen-cubic-foot cargo space of your SUV, he's the buddy you want to invite over. Beneath his blue-collar exterior there lives a logistics magician.

Craig Hite landed in the election warehouse after a shorter stint as truck driver and many years in the printing business, where he developed a knack for tinkering with balky equipment. As St. Louis County's aging voting machines got crankier, that skill paid off. He describes much of the work done by warehouse employees as a repetitive *Groundhog Day* grind, but with a mission. "We're in the background, behind the curtain, but we're a big part of the show," he said. "My old truck driving adage was, 'if the wheels ain't turning, you ain't earning.' So, we've got to keep the wheels turning out here to keep things going."

Winter and Hite started the warehouse cleanout by creating a disassembly line. I could hear it before I saw it: hammers banging, drills whirring, liberated metal parts clanging onto the concrete floor. The sounds jarred the otherwise quiet, white-collar offices just beyond the warehouse door. From a distance, it sounded chaotic and possibly dangerous, but once inside, I could see the order—a cacophonous choreography of tool kits, rolling carts, and accumulating heaps of dismantled machinery.

Winter divided his workers into three teams. "They come in, they take everything off, all the wires, the power pack, the printer, all of it," he told me. "They're basically pounding them out. We've got the pedal to the metal." It was taking two weeks to take apart 250 DRE machines, and there were 1,800 of them. Simple math indicated that they had weeks more to go.

But they weren't merely dismantling the machines, chucking the pieces into dumpsters and trucking them to a landfill. They were sorting and recycling everything they could—metal panels, glass computer screens, electrical wiring, housings, switches, and even the screws, bolts, and nuts that had held it all together. Every component had a designated destination in one of the huge, heavy-duty cardboard boxes known in warehouse lingo as "Gaylords." Winter had labeled each one with the parts to be placed—"tossed" would be more accurate—inside.

Figuring out a way to dispose of the dismantled pieces responsibly was a challenge. Apparently, no company specializes in recycling voting machines. Electronics recyclers claim that they can do the job, but they want the whole machine—intact— which is a very pricey shipping proposition. The vendors bidding on St. Louis County's new system knew that, so some proposals included an added line-item charge for getting rid of the old equipment. One bidder explicitly excluded equipment disposal from its contract.

Getting rid of old voting equipment is a pesky problem everywhere in election world. "I have been to local election offices where old or decertified equipment is stacked almost literally to the ceiling because the jurisdiction can't use it but doesn't know where to send it next," wrote election expert Douglas Chapin, in an article describing the equipment-disposal problem facing Pennsylvania's Lackawanna County in 2016. That county's election manager stored outdated voting equipment in county warehouses and moved it three times before a local recycling company finally agreed to take it. "It's not quite ashes to ashes, but it is helpful to remember that today's purchases are future recycling fodder, or even garbage," observed Chapin.

Shipping out obsolete voting equipment intact is itself a risky proposition, especially if administrators are not careful about the information they leave on board. Media reports are rife with accounts of researchers who have tested the process by buying discarded voting equipment via eBay and other internet marketplaces. They've found that acquiring "EOL," meaning end-of-life voting equipment, is alarmingly easy. There are tons of used election machines floating around out there, much of it dumped whole, with fully loaded hard drives containing election results and even voter information.

"If getting voting machines delivered to my door was shockingly easy, getting inside them proved to be simpler still," wrote researcher Brian Varner in *Wired* in 2018. He reported buying used voting machines for just one hundred dollars. "The tamper-proof screws didn't work, all the computing equipment was still intact, and the hard drives had not been wiped. The information I found on the drives, including candidates, precincts, and the number of votes cast on the machine, was not encrypted. Worse, the 'Property Of' government labels were still attached, meaning someone had sold government property filled with voter information and location data online, at a low cost, with no consequences. It would be the equivalent of buying a surplus police car with the logos still on it."

With those concerns in mind, St. Louis County decided to dismantle its own equipment. "We had two main reasons. First, it would save a significant amount of money. And second, it would prevent our machines from falling into the wrong hands on the secondary market," Eric Fey told me, clearly in risk-mitigation mode. "The last thing we wanted was one of our machines showing up at the Defcon hacking conference, as has happened to some other jurisdictions."

As Winter's chop shop broke down the equipment, they divvied up the pieces among companies who could recycle or repurpose them. Most of the plastic components went to Quincy Recycle, which had a processing plant nearby. Wisconsin-based Global Tech Environmental took batteries. And Didion Orf, in St. Peters, Missouri, got most of the separated-out electronic components. "There were some plastic parts that we couldn't find a recycler for and had to landfill," Fey further explained.

One thing that refused to die, at least for a while, were the seemingly immortal, old metal transport cases. They held sets of election-day supplies, presorted for polling places and therefore not convenient to store anywhere else. So, they stayed, clogging up a back hallway that became a temporary shelter for the homeless, zombie cases.

The department tried to save money at every turn. If anyone out there had a use for the black plastic, foam-insulated carrying cases for the now-defunct M-100 scanners, they were available—all five hundred of them—on a government-surplus site called GovDeals.com. The department eventually reaped a little more than $1,500 for them.

■

Then, as the warehouse gradually emptied out, the gears started to mesh in the boardroom, and the delivery date of new equipment became imminent. By the time the contract and financing decision finally came down, Fey and Stream found themselves in a hurry: A special election in November offered an opportunity to pilot the new system, but it was already early

September. They'd have to move quickly to get the new gear ready. Luckily, the limited-scope election would require only thirty polling places—out of the normal, countywide election complement of four hundred—making it an ideal time for a shakedown of the new system and the tweaked procedures that would accompany it.

Wisely, the department asked Hart InterCivic for an initial, partial delivery, with the balance to come immediately after the special election. That strategy gave them a chance to think some things out, such as how to reorganize the warehouse. But even with that limited first-wave delivery, there was a lot to do.

"I had many sleepless nights, just dwelling over how we were going to get this all done," said Hite. Dozens of trucks began backing up to the four loading bays within weeks of the contract signing. They arrived on a planned, every-other-day schedule, creating a whack-a-mole scenario: As soon as they unwrapped and sorted out one load, the next one arrived, sometimes before they were finished with the first.

I visited the warehouse as the first trucks began disgorging their cargo. Everything was on pallets, shrink-wrapped in layers of plastic, encased in wooden crates, and protected by multiple inches of molded foam buffers. The first challenge was to deal with the space-devouring packaging itself.

"You wouldn't believe the amount of byproduct that comes with this system," said Hite. "There's more of it than there is equipment. They don't tell you that when they sell it to you."

To keep up with the rapidly accumulating piles of packing materials, he had to make special arrangements with the department's trash hauler for extra dumpsters and more frequent pickups. And many more Gaylord boxes.

"We had to keep churning, or we would be buried in Styrofoam and packing debris, and there wouldn't be room for the next delivery dump," said Christian Tolbert, whose job as deputy director includes overseeing warehouse operations. Outside the loading dock, weeks after the last of the initial deliveries, there were still blue dumpsters overflowing with splintery scraps of torn-apart plywood packing crates, waiting for pickup.

"That was one of the few things we couldn't recycle. Nobody wanted that cheap plywood," Rick Stream reported to the board of commissioners, when they pointedly inquired about recycling. There were also no takers for the yards of sticky safety tape that held doors and compartments closed during transport, the hundreds of little packets of silica thrown in to keep moisture out, or the twist ties that held wires together and sealed up plastic bags containing small parts.

Navigating around the recycling bins and the now-naked new equipment, Winter and Hite had to keep tabs on what they had received and direct traffic so that everything ended up where it was supposed to be, without creating bottlenecks and twelve-cart pileups. Like generals deploying troops and materiel, they designated staging areas for each type of equipment and waited for the next round of incoming. Most smaller jurisdictions probably don't need as much military precision in the supply line, but a similar attention to detail is critical no matter the size of the operation.

They studied the available space, took measurements, and sketched out a complete reboot of the floor plan. The goal was to find the perfect spot for each item and create a logical sequence for loading, unloading, and storage. They had eighteen thousand square feet to do it in. As warehouses go, that's not a lot. It was going to be a tight fit. Even at this early phase, Winter was mapping out aisles, rows, and stacks, assigning every parking spot a locator number that would match up with a specific storage container and the equipment inside. Slowly but surely, he was creating a matrix of blue masking tape on the floor, each strip scrawled with the code for its slot. A more permanently marked set of labels would come later to formalize the new floor plan.

Winter was grateful to have the partial delivery to experiment with. Less than a week after the upcoming special election, he would be shifting into overdrive, when the rest of the shipment was scheduled to arrive. "We would be getting one full semitrailer truckload per day for several weeks. We were going to have our hands full," said Tolbert.

Hite's and Winter's warehouse operation is quite different than those in some other—usually much smaller—jurisdictions, Eric Fey told me. "I know one election clerk who has only a few voting machines," he said. "They store them in the attic of the courthouse above their office. Another one's got a storage shed across the court square. In some jurisdictions, you would be hard-pressed to figure out where any of it is."

■

On election day, voters probably don't focus on how much equipment it takes to supply a polling place. We just want someone to hand us a ballot, direct us to a voting machine, and get us in and out as quickly as possible. But the warehouse crew knows that to run an election, in addition to the obvious things—poll pads, printers, scanners, and ballot boxes—you need a truckload of other essentials. Polling sites need signs telling voters where to park and where to enter. They need printer paper, extra toner, extension cords; a passel of pens, pencils, paper clips, and staplers; cellphone chargers; packets of special voting forms, envelopes, and voter-information charts to hang on the wall; and, of course, a United States flag. Running out of paper clips may not be as disruptive as running out of ballots, but voters notice when an election operation seems sloppy or underprepared. Even little details, like being able to attach important documents together, are part of guaranteeing election security and voter confidence. In St. Louis County, consistency means delivering the identical set of supplies to four hundred locations. A standardized packing system is crucial.

Across the country, election managers have created a wide variety of systems for making sure all the "stuff" gets out to polling places. Some do this better than others, and in many locations, election setup consists of a lone worker tossing ballots and supplies into the back of a car and hauling them to a polling site. In St. Louis County, nobody remembers exactly when the metal transport cases came into play, but by 2019, everybody was ready for something more capacious, more easily maneuvered, and better looking, with a lock that worked and doors that weren't so warped that you had to karate-kick them open. An intensive product search yielded a solution: heavy-duty, six-foot-tall, lockable, metal cages-on-wheels.

Buying them was the first move. Deciding how to pack them took some intense mental gymnastics. On the floor in front of a prototype, Winter and Hite gathered a full kit of the election-day supplies needed for a typical polling place. "We just stared at it all for a while, until we started seeing how it could all fit inside," Winter told me.

"If you've ever played *Tetris*, you know what it was like," said Hite. One puzzle piece at a time, he and Winter started loading, unloading, turning, fitting and refitting, until they cajoled everything into place. They got helpful input from many sources, especially the people who would train poll workers on how to off-load the equipment and supplies at polling places, unsupervised, and then put it all back at the end of the day. Satisfied with their scheme, they created a storyboard of photos showing Winter positioning items in the cage. They glued copies into every cage in the fleet, along with detailed printed instructions. The result is a polling-place-in-a-box that's the same for every precinct.

"It's a good plan, but you have to wonder how well poll workers will stick to it at the end of their fourteen-hour shift on a busy election day," one of those trainers, Kevin McCloskey, told me. "It will be interesting to see how close to the picture they are when they come back, or if everything is just jammed in."

A few weeks later, after the special election in which they beta-tested the new cages, he got his answer. "Most of them were picture perfect," said Hite. "But some of the pollworker teams just barely managed to cram everything in and get the door closed. A few, when we opened them up, exploded like snakes-in-a-can."

Unfortunately, Winter's packing prowess had unintentionally created a monster. A cage fully loaded with all the printers, scanners, poll pads, and supplies needed for one polling place weighed around seven hundred pounds, about the same as four full kegs of beer. The packed-up cages would be nearly immovable objects—even for the well-muscled people who deploy equipment—if Hite hadn't decided to scrounge some additional budget bucks to retrofit the cages with heavier-duty wheels.

The bulk and weight of the new cage system also necessitated a new reconnaissance mission for—who else—the mapping guys/polling-place wranglers. They needed to revisit every one of the district's four hundred polling sites. Their assignment was to assess parking lots, door openings, and hallway widths to make sure delivery crews could muscle the behemoths along gravel paths, over bumpy thresholds, through the short, narrow doors of old church buildings, and down carpeted school passageways, without tipping them over or damaging floors.

As I began to understand the scope of work handled by warehouse employees, I was surprised to learn that, including Hite and Winter, there were only eleven full-timers. Most of the workers had been there for years. The most recent new hire, Hite told me, was six years ago. The same nine guys who rearranged the warehouse, unpacked the new equipment, broke down the old machines, screwed together the transport cages, loaded them up with supplies, and swept debris off the warehouse floor are also the trusted drivers who deploy the equipment before election day and gather it up in the days after.

Warehouse guys do more than just pick up and drop off. They have an election-integrity role, too, in making sure the right stuff arrives, unmolested, at the right place, and then securing it against on-site tampering. Once they've rolled the cages into position at a polling site, St. Louis County's drivers immobilize them by threading heavy-duty cables between the wheels and padlocking them in place.

Not every jurisdiction takes that extra step. Enterprising reporters from news outlets around the country have documented many instances of voting machines left unsecured in hallways outside polling sites, both before and after elections. "Some jurisdictions just deliver the equipment a couple of days before election and leave it out," said Eric Fey, disapprovingly.

For Hite's delivery crew, most drop-offs are routine: roll the transport cages into a rented truck; tie them down; drive to designated polling sites; and push them to an agreed-upon spot to await unpacking on election day. Just before the March 2020, Missouri primary election, I followed along as driver Ryan Hunt, accompanied by his helper, Eric Fey, delivered equipment to ten locations. Some of them required uphill maneuvering and a final, extra-energy shove to get the 700-pound cage over a raised threshold. Volunteers at several sites were setting up for fish-fry dinners and directed Hunt and Fey to put the equipment in a corner where it wouldn't interfere with the buffet line or take up table space.

Equipment delivery can be hazardous, too. Election staffer Zach Goldford accompanied a crew as it was wheeling a transport cage into an elementary school. "Are you the bird people?" asked a school staff member, thinking that they were with a wildlife conservation group that was giving a presentation to the students that day. Then, as the elections crew positioned the cage in the gym, one of the wildlife organization's falcons got loose. "It was flying and flapping all around us," said Goldford. "Fortunately, the falcon handler coaxed the bird back into its own cage. But that was pretty scary."

Having managed the same routes for years, St. Louis County drivers also have become experts on their locations. "They know the people. They know the pastors of the churches or the leader of the community center, which door to go in, and where the equipment goes," said Hite. "They start their deliveries six days before countywide elections, and they decide on the delivery sequence themselves, based on their knowledge of the sites. They can say, 'Okay, well this school or this church is closed on Thursday. There's nobody there, so I need to make sure that's a Friday delivery or Wednesday delivery.' So, they do all the navigating with those things in mind."

That knowledge adds value, said Hite, who shared with me his vision of a warehouse increasingly integrated into overall operations. Warehouses tend to be the stepchildren of many corporate operations. Not that many years ago, St. Louis County's election warehouse was in a separate building. And even when the department moved to its current location, where the warehouse is on site, previous supervisors were in the habit of protecting their sovereignty, enforcing an unspoken, but understood Berlin Wall between warehouse and administrative offices.

Hite has been breaking down that barrier. The swift change-over to new equipment has helped his plan along. As new equipment landed in the warehouse, needing mandatory acceptance testing, it was all hands on deck. Much of the administrative office population crossed over into the warehouse to help do the technical intake, creating awareness and mutuality on both sides.

Warehouse workers played a key role in pre-election processing in 2020. Running every poll pad, printer, and scanner through a prescribed testing routine, they made sure that equipment was synching properly, performing its functions correctly, getting a full electrical charge, and had all of the necessary connectors.

At least one veteran warehouse worker viewed the job as part of a bigger picture. "People use these machines to tell their elected officials what they want. It's a big part of our democracy," said Tim Peterson. "We're maintaining the tools that give people a voice. It's important work."

Hite also sees a potential role for warehouse employees as site evaluators. "Maybe we could be eyes and ears, know which locations work and which don't—be recognized as more of a liaison, maybe even do site reconnaissance and relieve the mapping guys of that added job," he said. "It might give our warehouse guys more of an incentive, more of a face in the overall operation, take them out of the shadows."

Early in 2020, Hite's vision began moving closer to reality, when Christian Tolbert announced at a board meeting that the warehouse was getting an identity upgrade. "We're changing the name to 'logistics,'" said Tolbert. "With all of the work they do on equipment and in getting things to the right place at the right time, logistics is a better reflection of their role."

Chances are, as time goes on, there won't be a lot of shadows —or any place to hide, even if they wanted to. While 2019 was a big year for election warehouses, 2020 and beyond could be even bigger. Latecomers to the nationwide, equipment-replacement surge will be scrambling to meet immovable election deadlines. And although Winter and Hite can thank their administrative higher-ups for thinking ahead and giving them the gift of time, they still face many hurdles, many of which may come as surprises. With their small staff and a tight election schedule, there is never an off-season.

8

Sleuths

Out of more than one billion ballots cast between 2000 and 2014, there were thirty-one credible instances of voter-impersonation fraud. It is more likely that an American will be struck by lightning than that he will impersonate another voter at the polls.

–The Brennan Center for Justice,
"The Myth of Voter Fraud," 2018

"I'M AN EXPERT AT SCRIBBLES. I used to teach preschool," said Marie Ellison. That ability—to read the unreadable—is a special skill that makes Ellison particularly valuable at election headquarters, where illegibility is an occupational hazard.

In elections, signatures count. Just ask Ellison's teammate, Linda McLain. Or Peggy Kochner. Or Theresa Dintleman. Their jobs are all about signatures. They live on the dotted line, next to the *X*, in the blank box where you inscribe—or more likely, scrawl—your John Hancock. You may never meet them, but you won't get very far as a voter, a candidate, or a petition-circulator if you can't get past them, or people who have jobs like theirs where you vote.

Signatures and personal marks have been a part of human culture for centuries. Archaeologists have unearthed clay tablets with carved-in tags dating back more than three thousand years. There's evidence of signed work in the Roman Empire. In 1677, the British Parliament passed a law requiring signatures on contracts, creating a precedent that formalized the legal status of signatures, and then spread throughout the world.

In legalese, your signature is a "commonly understood acclamation of assent." In plain English, that means that your signature is a guarantee—an affirmation that you are who you say you are, that you've read what you're signing, that you agree to the terms of engagement, and as Alexander Hamilton (the Broadway version) said, it means you were "in the room where it happened." Writing your name on a document—known in legal circles as your "manuscript signature"—is an oath. Ellison, McLain, Kochner, Dintleman and others who work with them, each in their own way, are the sleuths who make sure that people who sign election-related documents are for real.

Participating in elections starts with registering to vote. But just as there is no consistency in how we vote in the US, there's no universal way to register either. Like everything else related to voting, it's a state-by-state process. North Dakota is the only state where you don't have to register to vote. For the rest of the country, depending on where you live, you might register in person, by mail, or online. In an increasing number of states, you can be automatically registered to vote when you renew your driver's license. Some voting-rights activists have been pushing a plan in which people would be automatically registered to vote on their eighteenth birthdays.

Deadlines for registering to vote vary widely, too. Most states require between eight- and thirty-days' advance notice, but even that is changing. In twenty-one states plus the District of Columbia, you can walk in on election day and both register and vote, and more states are joining the same-day-registration movement. In fact, election experts increasingly view advance deadlines for voter registration as antiquated.

The history of voter registration in America is not pretty. Rather than coming from an idealistic, inclusive philosophy, voter registration has often been a tool of exclusion—a practice that, unfortunately, persists today in some states. Voter registration first gained wide popularity in the nineteenth century, as politicians sought ways to keep people of color, poor people, and immigrants—people they viewed as undesirable—from participating in elections and eroding the power of white, wealthy men. There were, however, some positive effects: Defining who could vote and who couldn't—whether these criteria were fair or not—created clarity, which helped calm things down on election days in the late 1800s, when it was not uncommon for there to be riots at polling places over who could vote.

Overall in voter registration, four basic rules apply. You must be a US citizen; meet your state's residency requirements (you can be homeless and still meet these criteria); be eighteen years old on or before election day; and be registered by your state's deadline. And one more thing: You must sign your voter registration application.

But whether you sign up at the Social Security office, at your local DMV, at a registration booth at a charity run/walk, or in your pajamas on the couch with a laptop, filling out an application is just the opening move. You're not registered until someone official says you are.

In St. Louis County, that's where Linda McLain, squiggle-expert Marie Ellison, and the rest of their team come in. They're the signature sentinels. McLain has been at this job for a decade, plowing through the piles of incoming registrations that pour in year-round, each needing individual processing to become official. Some are easy, with everything filled out and written in perfectly formed, unmistakable letters. But some are much more difficult, and McLain has seen it all: illegible, incomplete, rainspotted, crumpled, or mangled from waiting too many weeks in the bottom of a procrastinator's overstuffed briefcase.

McLain's job is not for paper- or process-phobic people. When the mail comes in, she rubber-bands registration cards into batches of twenty-five. In 2018, her department received 45,187 new registrations and more than 115,000 address and/or name changes, yielding megabatches. Moving the applications along is a painstaking, step-by-step job.

"Fortunately, most are complete," McLain told me. "But some people forget to sign, or miss the checkbox indicating that they're US citizens. We follow up on that, usually with a letter. If you signed up on your phone or on a tablet, which a lot of people do, you may not have a signature that we can count as valid. In that case, we send a form for them to sign and send back. Until we have all the required information, the voter is in 'pending' status. We try our best to get every application complete, whether it's a new registration, a change of address or name, or a duplicate submitted by someone who doesn't remember that they're already registered or thinks—mistakenly—that they have to register again for every election."

Of the 45,000-plus applications received in 2018, McLain's team disqualified 808. Eric Fey estimated that between 10,000 and 20,000 of that year's voter registration applications were duplicates submitted by people already on the rolls.

What a fourth-grade teacher might call "penmanship" does indeed count, but common sense is the guiding principle, McLain told me. Reportedly, some jurisdictions elsewhere have used an exact-match signature policy as a tool of disenfranchisement. In those jurisdictions, on election day, if the signature of record doesn't exactly match what the voter inscribes on the poll pad or in a precinct book, their vote can be flagged and potentially not counted. That tactic can exclude people who, in the years since they first signed a voter registration card, may have developed arthritis or neurological disorders that affect their ability to write. Younger voters can find themselves excluded, too, because they've become accustomed to signing casually with a finger or a stylus, making them less likely to have a fixed signature.

"We're encountering a lot of young voters who were never taught cursive writing, so they print their names in block letters. They don't have what most of us would call a signature. But it counts anyway. Even an *X* is considered valid," said Eric Fey.

Daniel Smith, a professor of political science at the University of Florida, studied signature rejections on vote-by-mail ballots and reported that younger voters were four times more likely to have their absentee ballots rejected than voters over sixty-five, whose signatures are more set.

"That's not what we do here," McLain said. "We do look at the original signature when a voter makes a change to their record, to see if it matches up. But we're aware that the way you signed ten years ago is going to be a little different than your current signature. We're not official handwriting experts, but your signature is still going to have something distinctive, like the way you make your *B* or your *L*s, so that's going to stand out."

In addition, McLain's team uses "wet" signatures as points of comparison when voters make changes using online forms. "Your wet signature is one that you signed with a real writing implement, a signature that we have from your earlier records," said Kim Creswell, a supervisor in the voter registration section. "Some voters have four or five signatures on file from address or name changes they've filed before. We can use those as the base."

There's a mission behind these machinations, and it's clear that the people who do the work get it. Asked about the purpose behind her job, Creswell jumped in with palpable passion: "Our goal is to make sure that people who qualify to register can do it. We do everything we can to get them registered, so they have their right to go vote. We are sworn deputies, sworn to uphold the law. We have official badges to prove it." Any election director would see that attitude as mission buy-in to die for.

Responsiveness is important to voters, too. St. Louis County voter registration workers try to send confirmation of every completed registration within about ten days. But when they get swamped by applications close to the deadline, it can take longer, and they don't control the US Postal Service. For voters who may have gone out of their way to register, or who have at long last made good on a promise to their mom to opt in, the wait can seem endless. Workers on phone duty close to election day field many calls from rankled people who haven't received their notifications. Fortunately, in most states, anybody with access to a computer and the internet can verify their status by going to their secretary of state's website and clicking on the handy "Check Your Registration" feature.

It wasn't always this way. Statewide voter registration databases are a relatively new development. They became mandatory when Congress passed HAVA in 2002. More recently, states got together to form a voluntary, nonprofit group called the Electronic Registry Information Center (ERIC). More than half of US states participate, Missouri included. It's not a national voter registration database. ERIC is an information clearinghouse that compares states' data to information kept by the US Postal Service and to death records held by Social Security. It tackles the problem of keeping up with a voting population that is constantly changing, as people move, change their names, or die. According to ERIC, as many as one in every eight voter registration records is inaccurate. Given recent government reports showing that Russian hackers probed the voter rolls in virtually every state, keeping a close watch on the lists is more essential than ever.

That threat makes backup a critical security measure, and, in a way, there's an app for that. In St. Louis County, the team scans every voter registration and transforms it into a PDF file. "We do that for every voter," said McLain. "So, we have a digital picture of everything the voter filled out."

As a hard backup, they save every voter registration card. A monster-sized filing cabinet called the Lektriever takes up an entire wall near the voter registration team's section of the office. It looks vaguely like a commercial baking oven, with rotating shelves that serve as the repository not for freshly baked croissants but for registration cards received in recent years. They're grouped by batches, in the order received, and stored in trays in the Lektriever. But the Lektriever does not have infinite space. It fills up after five to seven years. That's when the cleanout and alphabetizing begin. Alphabetizing is, quite possibly, the least-loved activity in the office.

"If you don't look busy, you might get a tray of cards to be sorted," Melissa Moore told me. For walk-ins who want to absentee vote in person, drop off paperwork, or gain admittance to the inner sanctum for a meeting, Moore, a professional-looking presence at the front desk, is the first person they encounter. "Melissa is our first line of defense," another staffer told me. "She works really hard to make sure everyone gets what they need."

During one of my visits to the office, Moore was slowly working her way through a three-foot-long pack of *B*s from 2012. I declined her offer to set me up with my own tray of voting cards to alphabetize.

"Everybody alphabetizes," said Moore, who has worked in the department for nearly thirty-six years. It is probably one of the things that the dreaded "other duties as assigned" refers to on the department's job descriptions. When the cards are finally in proper *ABC* order, they're packed up in boxes and sent to the county's central records center, where they're scanned onto microfilm for future reference.

St. Louis County's voter registration regimen may not be an exact match for what happens in other jurisdictions, but some universal principles apply. The Election Assistance Commission (EAC) puts it this way: "Maintaining an accurate voting roll enfranchises voters because it lowers the likelihood of lines at the polls, reduces voter confusion and decreases the number of provisional ballots."

Marie Ellison has a more down-to-earth explanation of the work: "Nobody wants to be the person who keeps someone from voting by getting one number wrong. If I'm not doing my job correctly, it messes up everything in the chain."

■

In a nearby section of the office, Peggy Kochner wrestles with her own subset of signatures. She supervises absentee voting, a convenience viewed in today's highly mobile culture as a given, but one that was rare before the Civil War. That was when northern states began to see an advantage to allowing soldiers fighting for the Union to vote for it, too. Absentee voting then grew dramatically during World War I, when three million potential voters served overseas. The idea caught on, presumably because it seemed the fair thing to do, and by 1918, historians report, nearly every state had a system that allowed men serving in the military to cast a ballot while away from home. Not long after that, more than twenty states began permitting people to vote absentee if they could demonstrate a work-related reason for being out of town on election day.

Today, absentee voting is a critical but much misunderstood aspect of elections. Many voters mistakenly believe that absentee ballots don't count unless the election results are close. Election administrators everywhere are constantly debunking that myth.

"Every absentee vote counts just the same as an in-person vote," Kochner said. In St. Louis County, rather than becoming lost in the election-day shuffle or held back and brought in like the cavalry at the last minute, they are the first partial-vote totals reported to the public after the polls close on election day. "The polls close at 7 p.m., and we report the absentee totals at 7:01," said Eric Fey.

Peggy Kochner is a no-nonsense, straight talker who has worked at election headquarters for seventeen years. She's genetically inclined, it seems, for the job. Her mother Rosemary, a fixture in the department for decades, tutored many novice administrators in the art of elections. She retired in

2000. Peggy, who previously worked as a business journalist, came on board in 2002, after some coaxing from her mom.

Kochner's desk is smothered in paper as she works her way through the mounds of absentee-ballot requests that demand her close attention. Before she okays an application, Kochner or another staffer checks the voter database to make sure the applicant is registered and then compares signatures, using the same commonsense principles at work in the neighboring voter registration department.

People can be quite curious about the signature situation, Kochner told me. "We had a guy call us a few years ago who said he was formerly with the FBI or the Secret Service," she said. "He wanted to know about the signatures. He said, 'Can you please connect me to your signature specialist?'" Kochner said she leaned back in her chair, covered the phone's mouthpiece and called out to the room, "Hey, do we have a signature specialist?" "That got a laugh from the other people in the office," she added. "I told the caller, 'We're all signature specialists here.'"

Kochner is always on the alert for fraudulent applications and ballots. "There are a lot of opportunities to cheat in absentee voting," she said, although she declined to be specific. But many election researchers say that cases of voter-impersonation fraud are rare. One red flag, though, would be getting a request to deliver multiple absentee ballots to one address, Eric Fey told me.

Another potential scenario is known as ballot harvesting. An Associated Press news report offered a notable example that allegedly occurred in a very close North Carolina congressional race in 2018: "Political operatives may have collected unsealed absentee ballots and either manipulated them or threw out ballots from minority voters who might otherwise have gone to the polls." The alleged ploy resulted in criminal indictments for five people. In addition, because the outcome of the contest may have been affected by the scheme, the state ordered a revote.

St. Louis County experienced a similar incident in 2016. Voters in Berkeley, a municipality within the county, alleged that their mayor had unlawfully told them to leave their absentee ballots unsealed. Then, he picked them up and mailed them in. Those allegations prompted St. Louis County police and the FBI to send monitors to watch election workers open the absentee ballots from some Berkeley precincts. They found some irregularities that appeared to benefit the mayor and his allies. In 2019, citing a pattern of ballot harvesting over several years, a special prosecutor indicted the Berkeley mayor, charging him with four felony counts of election fraud and one felony count of forgery.

That was a case that Kochner probably knew about but didn't want to discuss when we talked, because it was still under investigation. In her many years in the department, she has learned so much about absentee chicanery that she's thinking about writing a murder mystery in which election fraud plays a role.

A visit to her workspace reveals that the primary décor on the wall behind her is a large whiteboard, emblazoned with large, handwritten red numbers indicating critical deadlines in the absentee timeline: opening day for ballot requests; last day for ballot requests; deadline for completed absentee ballots to land in election headquarters. These are reference points that Kochner and other staffers will need to repeat, possibly thousands of times, to inquiring callers during each election cycle.

"The most stressful days are probably the last day we're allowed to mail out ballots and the day after that," said Amy Blankenship, who used to work in absentee, but is now head of human resources. She still helps Kochner during peak times. "You're racing against the clock. People are very upset that they can no longer vote by mail. They call in, some of them screaming and yelling, so you're having to calm them down. It's a tough time."

Kochner is a matter-of-fact person in the morally ambiguous world of absentee voting in Missouri. To vote absentee in Missouri, you must give a reason and put your signature on a declaration, which is essentially signing an affidavit. The only acceptable excuses are absence from the jurisdiction on election day; working as an election official on election day; physical disability or illness; religious practice; incarceration; or certified participation in Missouri's address-confidentiality program because of safety concerns. If you simply want to avoid long lines on election day, or just want the convenience of voting at home, or if you try to use "I'm working that day" as an excuse, you're outside the legal limits. As of early 2020, Missouri was one of only ten states that have not yet enacted no-excuse absentee voting.

"Missouri's absentee laws make liars out of a lot of voters," said Kochner. For the November 2018 midterms, St. Louis County took in more than 54,000 absentee ballots, or about 12 percent of the total ballots cast. In addition to mailed-in or dropped-off absentee ballots, the county allows in-person absentee voting at headquarters and at several temporary satellite locations for a short period of time just before election day. But they are quick to remind everyone that it's not early voting, which is a completely different animal, and it's not allowed in the Show-Me State.

In November 2018, more than half of the absentee vote in St. Louis County was done in-person. Voters declared their excuses on the spot, as election staffers looked on and watched them indicate an excuse on the poll pad. Kochner is careful to avoid saying that election officials wink at the deception. "We just let them know that they have to pick one of the reasons," she said. "When forced to select one, almost everyone chooses 'absent on election day.'"

One category of voters who don't need to fib are people who live overseas or are serving in the military. A federal law, known as UOCAVA, ensures their right to vote. Under a unique law passed in Texas in 2000, even astronauts out of town—off the planet—on a space flight can vote absentee.

In St. Louis County, military and overseas absentee applications—signatures required—drop on Beau Coker's desk just across the aisle from Kochner. They have deadlines, too, although there's a special grace period for military voters deployed in war zones. Coker keeps a world-map tab open on his computer monitor. The color purple designates countries where he has sent an absentee application. When I looked at it in 2019, there were 106 purple countries.

"I've gotten an education in world geography on this job," said Coker, who joined the department in 2017. For the high-volume November 2018 midterm, he sent out nearly sixteen hundred absentee ballots to military and overseas voters and received about one thousand in time to be counted. Some of them contained handwritten thank-you notes from voters grateful to be able to participate in the election. Sometimes, he gets a thank-you email. Coker keeps a sampling of them taped to his desk, to remind himself that what he's doing makes a difference. "They mean a lot to me," he said. "I'm just here doing my job, but I'm glad I can help them get their vote in."

■

Until 2017, it took a village—virtually everyone who worked at St. Louis County election headquarters—to mail out absentee ballots to voters qualified to receive them. "The process was absolutely crazy—a nightmare," deputy director Julie Leicht told me. Absentee ballots, just like election-day ballots, need to list the correct contests and issues for each voter—the proper ballot style. And, particularly in a countywide election for mayors, trustees, and city councils, there can be as many as three hundred different ballot styles to match up with qualified voters.

"We did it all manually. We'd have bipartisan teams working all day for days, identifying the voter's ballot style, pulling the right ballot, inserting it into the voter's envelope, matching the right label with the right envelope," said Leicht, shuddering as she recalls the nearly eighty thousand absentee ballots they sent out for the record-breaking 2008 presidential election. "It took forever, and we would all work overtime because we had a deadline to get it all out. You'd just want to run away."

Finally, after years of pressure-packed, late-night, error-prone chaos, computerization came to the rescue. "Now, as absentee applications come in, we send the information in batches, as database files, to a commercial printer, and they're able to do all of it much faster and with fewer mistakes. It has virtually eliminated human error," said Leicht, obviously relieved to have relinquished this soul-killing chore to a system that can churn out thirty thousand completed absentee mail-out packets in a single shift. The in-house, manual output was about three hundred per team per day. "It's a big win for us and for voters."

Of course, absentee voting has both outs and ins. A large percentage of the ballots that go out make the return trip as votes, and managing that flow is yet another labor-intensive job. A few years ago, as absentee voting gained popularity and grew from a trickle to a tidal wave, the department created, out of necessity, a job called "ballot opener." More recently, a machine took over the process of slicing open the absentee envelopes. From a distance, one might mistake it for the meat slicer in a supermarket's deli department.

But ballot openers—of the human variety—are still on the payroll, most of them as temps. They focus on processing the ballots, not tabulating the votes they contain. In presidential elections, the department might hire as many as one hundred ballot openers, who work hunched over tables crammed into any air pocket in the office. They operate in bipartisan twosomes. Their first job is to make sure that the envelopes have been properly signed—and, if required, notarized.

The signature requirement is a big deal: In 2008 in Minnesota, Al Franken beat Norm Coleman for a US Senate seat by a sliver, less than three hundred votes. In that race, almost four thousand absentee ballots were not counted because the envelope was not signed. The problem was a flaw in the design of the envelope: Voters didn't notice the signature line, an innocent mistake that ultimately disenfranchised them. That screwup prompted the Minnesota secretary of state's office to redesign the absentee mail-in envelope to include an outsized X to prominently indicate where voters should sign. In the 2010 election, the missing-signature total dropped to 837.

In St. Louis County, before the envelopes are opened, a scanner reads an identifying bar code imprinted on the envelope, generating a list of voters who have taken the absentee route. The information ends up on the precinct poll pads, where "Absentee Ballot Received" in the voter's record prevents a second, in-person vote. Ballot openers follow a precise sequence to make sure that they've processed every ballot and prepared it to be counted.

"It seems like a really simple job, but we have training classes for it because processing absentee ballots is so important," said Peggy Kochner, who, like everyone else in the core employee roster of about sixty workers, can be pulled off her desk and into whatever is the squeakiest wheel at any given moment in the election cycle.

Apparently, the training is working. One morning, before the March 2020 presidential primary, I observed a ballot-opening shift, with twelve teams of workers packed together in rows of six-foot tables. I was surprised at how quiet the room was. The predominant sound was a low hum of brief, on-task conversations between team members. It was evidence, I concluded, of the diligence and focus of under-the-radar temporary workers, who were taking a rote, repetitive job quite seriously.

"I try really hard to make sure I'm doing it correctly," one worker told me. "And actually, it's fun. You meet some new people, and a lot of the time, you click with your partner. Plus, I learn how things work."

Ballot opening is also a time-sensitive operation, and it can be a crunch. "You only have so many days when you're allowed to open them in Missouri, starting on the Thursday before an election. Once we start, we work Thursday, Friday, Saturday, even on a Sunday and then Monday, so they can start tabulating them on Tuesday, election day," Kochner explained.

That early-opening and election-day-counting window is a luxury not available in some other states. In Michigan, for example, by state law, absentee ballots cannot even be opened before the polls close on election day itself. "We're trying to get that changed before the 2020 presidential election," said a Michigan election official during a panel discussion at the 2020 EAC Summit. Anticipating a giant turnout—a high percentage of which is expected to come in via absentee voting—the administrator worried that being restricted to after-hours opening and tabulation of absentee ballots could cause Michigan's results to be delayed long into the night, if not into the next day. "We don't want to be Ohio," she said, teasing a Buckeye State colleague next to her on the panel, whose state has sometimes been among the last to report results in presidential elections.

During a ballot-opening shift just before a special election in 2019, one St. Louis County team showed me some of the envelopes they were working on. Most were routine and sailed through. But some lacked signatures and would require follow-up, if there was enough time before the election to reach the voter. One voter had cut off the bottom half of the ballot to make it fit in the envelope, rather than simply folding it. Several ballots displayed evidence of the meal the voter was eating or the coffee they were drinking as they filled in the ovals.

One duty of ballot openers is to smooth out the ballot so that it will go through the scanner and be read properly. But some absentee ballots arrive so badly mangled that they can't be processed in the normal way. One team showed me a ballot so crumpled and torn into so many pieces—presumably by a post-office machine—that it was delivered in a zip-sealed plastic sandwich bag, with a note from a postal worker that said, "Sorry." The team who received it diligently pieced it back together, puzzle-style, so that the reconstituted ballot could be duplicated on a copy machine and then scanned and added to the vote total.

"All in a day's work," said Beau Coker, who had drawn extra duty as a ballot opener that afternoon.

■

No one creates more need for signature sleuthing than people who circulate petitions—those clipboard-wielding activists who pursue you in supermarket parking lots, at festivals, and at political demonstrations. No matter where you live, for people pushing citizen-generated constitutional amendments, referendums, ballot initiatives, and even in some cases, their own candidacy, your signature is a hot commodity. As with everything else election related, requirements for the number of signatures vary, but one thing is universal: They need a lot. And what happens after you sign is another how-the-sausage-is-made story.

Recent developments have upped the ante for the signature police. Thirty-eight states allow citizens to bypass the legislature to make new laws or change old ones. Whether the cause is hyper-partisan politics, disaffection with do-nothing or do-too-much legislatures, or just a new-found love of direct democracy, election jurisdictions are seeing a surge in ballot issues and the signatures they generate. In 2018, there were

167 statewide measures on ballots in a total of thirty-one states. Some addressed big-ticket issues, like expanding voting rights for felons, reforming sentencing laws, or legalizing marijuana. In addition are the hundreds of hyper-local initiatives concerning smoking bans, or parking regulations, or other community-specific issues. Sometimes, the subjects are less serious, such as one proposal that would have allowed residents of a small Ohio town to keep miniature pigs as pets. But the signatures must be checked on the silly-sounding ones, too.

In St. Louis County, Theresa Dintleman is the petition signature verifier-in-chief. But she can't do the job alone, because the volume of ballot initiatives has ballooned: In 2016, the department received 42,900 pages of petitions, with ten signatures per page.

"People don't realize that we check every single signature, not a percentage, not a random sample," explained Dintleman, whose serene demeanor seems critical in a job that can require her and her team to wade through more than 400,000 signatures on a strict deadline. "Most of our workers can get through about 250 signatures in a day. In 2016, it took us nine weeks to complete the job."

That day rate works out to just thirty-one signatures per hour per worker—a very slow pace, it would seem. But, as the song says, you can't hurry love, and apparently, you can't hurry signature validation either. It's a meticulous procedure that Dintleman's team takes quite seriously.

The bottom line is to make sure that everyone who has signed meets two criteria: They're a registered voter in the state, and they live in the proper jurisdiction—congressional district, city, taxing district, school district or ward, for example—as required by the proposal. A legible signature is nice, but it's not enough. So, team members stop at each line on the signature sheet, red pen in hand, checking against the statewide voter registration database, sometimes applying data-search magic to get around indecipherable handwriting. When they're satisfied that the voter qualifies, they okay the signature and move on to the next.

It can be a mind-numbingly monotonous job. Some pages are problem free. But others have line after line of names that need special attention: addresses that don't match up; name changes that haven't been updated; chicken-scratch writing; common names that require them to scroll through a long list of John Smiths to find the one with a signature that resembles the one on the petition. "When you get a page full of those things, you want to tear your hair out. We keep trying, but by the end of your shift, you're cross-eyed," one worker told me.

"We're careful, and that slows things down," said Dintleman. "Sometimes the handwriting is sloppy because they're filling them out on a clipboard or rushing to get to a store, so it's difficult to read. But I tell the team, don't just go 'not registered' because you can't read it at first. You need to dive in there a little bit to try to find out, use every avenue. These people are out there signing on, and they want to be counted. We try every which way to find them in the database."

Typically, Dintleman's crew rejects about 25 percent of signatures on statewide petitions and about 9 percent on local ballot issues. Some signers aren't registered voters. Some are registered but live in the wrong district for the issue they're signing on to. Others may have changed their minds about signing and crossed out their names, or it may turn out that they've signed more than once, perhaps having forgotten that they'd already done so on a different day.

One candidate who learned about signatures the hard way was Barry Glantz, a local mayor who decided to run for a newly vacated seat on the St. Louis County Council. To secure a place on the ballot as an independent, a formula dictated by state law required him to get 1,284 valid signatures. He knocked on a lot of doors in his potential district, but that was slow going. Then, thinking that a local public water park in the district would be a target-rich environment, he and his wife set out, clipboards in hand, on a sweltering June afternoon, to garner as many signatures as they could. Unfortunately, Glantz didn't realize that many of the people splashing and watersliding did not live in his district. While he eventually managed to get more than 1,400 signatures—giving himself what he thought was a safe margin of error—more than a quarter of them didn't count. After what he called a "literally exhausting" process, he failed to reach the threshold and did not appear on the ballot.

Overshooting the quota is a smart strategy that usually pays off. But it makes more work for the people who inhabit the signature zone in election administrations. And one can imagine the frustration of finishing a massive signature-review project only to learn that your efforts have gone to waste—as has happened in many jurisdictions—when a lawsuit challenging the petitioner's issue convinces a judge to yank the whole thing from the ballot. For election workers, that is signature hell.

■

It may be tempting to think that pen-to-paper, wet signatures are going out of style, casualties of the digital age. That's a reasonable assumption, given how many businesses now accept electronic signatures for legal documents, bank deposits, package deliveries, or home repair services. Surely, goes the logic, something less vulnerable to forgery—such as a fingerprint or a retina scan—would make more sense to verify a voter's identity. But that idea apparently sounds too Orwellian to many legislators, as it relates to voting. So, it is probably a long way off.

In the nearer future, though, electronic signatures could make your handwritten autograph a relic of that quaint time known as the twenty-first century. In some states, lawmakers have proposed rules that allow electronic signatures on ballot initiatives and voter registration applications. But for most, concerns about election integrity have slowed the momentum. And even if manually inscribed signatures become extinct, new forms of signing-in will still require some form of double-checking. Some jurisdictions—particularly in states that have instituted vote-by-mail—are experimenting with signature-recognition software powered by artificial intelligence. St. Louis County isn't there yet, and neither are most jurisdictions. And that means job security for signature sleuths everywhere.

9

Glue

Austria's 2016 presidential election was postponed after adhesive seals on postal votes were found to have come unstuck. One political leader saw the problem as a metaphor for bigger issues in the country, saying "What we need most of all is for us to stick together."

–Guardian, *September 12, 2016*

AMY BLANKENSHIP HAS A corner office, but not the kind that corporate bigwigs covet. Hers is an oddly shaped space with no exterior windows, a niche that is more office-design afterthought than perk. But prestige and high visibility are not Blankenship's priorities. She oversees two decidedly non-glam functions in election world: money and personnel, putting her squarely among the back-office workers who rarely interact face-to-face with the public, who hold the fort on election day, and who provide the invisible glue that holds election administrations together.

Money, of course, is a key component of the connective tissue—the link that touches everything. The St. Louis County board of elections gets its annual operating budget of about

$9 million from the county government. But elections are extra and are expected to pay for themselves.

To fund its elections, the board estimates a cost—say, $2 million for a countywide municipal election—and divides up the total among the municipalities and taxing districts, proportionate to the registered voters that each encompasses. On top of that, there's a 5 percent surcharge, mandated by Missouri state statutes, that goes into a dedicated election services fund available for out-of-the-ordinary expenses. In addition, there's the equipment-usage fee that goes into yet another bucket, to accumulate money for voting equipment in the future. In the April 2018 municipal elections, the biggest bill went to the St. Louis County Community College District: $246,000. The smallest invoice went to a little municipality—Pacific, Missouri—whose .001 percent share of the registered voting population meant that it owed $7.58.

By Blankenship's calculations, the cost-per-vote in St. Louis County in November 2018 was about $1.15. By comparison, a North Dakota database lists that state's cost-per-vote for the same time period at $3.66. Does that mean that St. Louis County is more efficient? Not necessarily. Funding mechanisms, not surprisingly, vary from state to state and among local jurisdictions. Accordingly, it's hard to pin down election costs or to make meaningful comparisons. How much something "costs" can vary widely among states and between different counties within a single state.

"A larger county may pay less per ballot for printing costs than a smaller county because of economies of scale," goes the explanation on the National Conference of State Legislatures' website. "And a smaller county may have no problem recruiting and paying poll workers, whereas this may be a complicated and expensive proposition for a larger county." Some states have passed legislation to more accurately identify election costs, but we are a long way from a standardized way to collect and compare expenditures. Comparisons rely mostly on estimations and guess work.

Blankenship obsessively sorts her election-related beans via multiple databases, following complex money-handling rules dictated by state and county statutes. She does it all using a single small computer screen, unlike many others at neighboring workstations, who have two, three, or even four monitors. The IT department has offered her more. She told them not to bother. Her minimalist approach to a complex operation works for her. Apparently, it works for the department, too, because for the past few years, the election board has refunded $500,000 or more back to county government at the end of each fiscal year.

Blankenship has put in fourteen years in St. Louis County, steadily working her way through several departments and, most recently, adding human resources to her portfolio when that position became available. What's more enjoyable, hiring or counting? She didn't say. Numbers don't have daycare issues. But people are infinitely intriguing to Blankenship. So, it's probably a challenging daily mix.

Having a well-managed and happy workforce is important in any organization, but it's especially critical in election administration, said Blankenship. The department's relatively small workforce manages an operation with many moving parts and a big community impact.

"We have to stick together to make it all work," she said. "In other kinds of organizations or companies, you don't always get to see the big picture. You just do your little piece. You're a cog in the machine, and you don't know what the machine's doing. You don't see the end product. That's not what it's like around here. Everyone here experiences election day."

Just to make sure, in recent years the department has shipped out every new hire—whatever their level—to a polling place on the first election day that rolls around. "Everybody needs to understand what we are doing, what happens on election day, and how important that is," she explained. "I think, when it comes down to it, we all see ourselves as part of something bigger."

Maybe that sense of mission is why some workers stay for many years. "There's also a bonding factor," Blankenship added. "I think we get comfortable here. You kind of look at this as your second family. You're here with these people all day. Then during presidential election years, it feels like you live here. You're just working so many extra hours. You get to know everybody. You know about their families. What they did on the weekends. We have decent benefits. The pay is good. The work environment's good. For the most part, there's no reason to leave. I suspect that people who apply to work here have heard good things because we get at least ten applicants for every job we post."

When Blankenship described the pay as "good," she did not mean "great." Pay ranges in St. Louis County start at $9 per hour for a temporary employee. The entry-level pay for a senior clerk is $15.54 per hour. A poll-worker coordinator told me that their job pays in the lower end of the $30,000 range. Among salaried employees, an administrative assistant might start at $40,500, and a newly hired assistant director would get a minimum of $50,800. The department's top jobs—directors of elections—start at $100,899 and can rise to a maximum of $161,000.

By comparison—to the extent that comparisons are apples-to-apples—North Carolina's state director of elections will earn $140,000 in 2020. In a late 2019 job posting for the job of elections and voter registration manager, Snohomish County, Washington, listed an annual salary range of $86,000 to $121,000. A new systems and security supervisor in Pinellas County, Florida, walks in at between $70,000 and $75,000. Salary ranges are all over the place. One can spend hours scanning the listings on the Election Officials National Job Board and still not get a handle on how job classifications work or on best-versus-worst pay rates.

"The main reason employees give for leaving our department is salary," said Fey. He, Rick Stream and the board of directors are powerless in the pay scale department. They can ask; they can push. But it's up to the almighty county council to decide on compensation.

One of the department's highly valued IT professionals quit in December 2019, when a mushrooming election-technology company made him a salary offer he couldn't refuse. There is a good chance that his replacement will come from within—from a deep pool of seasoned, mission-ready talent.

Notably, if the department does need to reach beyond its own cadre of workers, it faces a hurdle created by Missouri statutes. New hires must be registered voters and residents of the jurisdiction, in this case St. Louis County, for at least one year before taking a job in elections.

"That's a big limitation," Fey told me. "We can't hire someone from a different county who may have the exact election-related experience we need. I'd like to see that law changed."

■

More than one person I interviewed called their own department "the glue," probably, I surmised, not because they viewed their work as the most important, but because they saw the connections between their jobs and other functions.

Perhaps the most glue-ish is Rosemarie Moss. Officially, she's the administrative assistant to Rick Stream. He's not the first director she's worked for—she's seen them come and go in her twenty-three years in the office. She could probably write her own book of election-department anecdotes and war stories, but she seems far too discreet for that. However, when coworkers want to know how to do something, where to find something, or when something happened back in the day, she's the encyclopedia. Her desk, situated prominently outside the director's office, is not just a workstation, it's an office-supply hub, a customer-service call center, and a medicine chest. Wedged in among the requisite keyboard, dual monitors, and phone is an assortment of the little things that office workers have asked her for over the years, the answers to "Hey, Rosemarie, do you happen to have …"

She does: a tangle of paper clips; a clump of rubber bands; tissues; scissors; staples; extra pens and pads of paper; and small bottles of hand sanitizer in scents preferred by her customers. Ask anyone to name the office Mom, and the answer will be "Rosemarie."

It seems that nobody walks by Moss's desk without stopping to ask a question, pick up an apothecary item, or just say good morning. Sometimes, a frustrated coworker will head over to request Moss's help with a difficult caller.

"I take the tough ones," she told me. "Apparently, I have a sedative effect on irate people."

Of Moss's many roles, perhaps the most obscure to the voting public is that of certifying ballot information for the municipal elections held every April. It entails making sure that information destined for the ballot comes in on time, is accurate, and is spelled and worded properly—election essentials that voters take for granted unless, of course, they notice something amiss. The job is part editor, part ballot cop, and part quality-control manager, with a dollop of coach and relaxation therapist thrown in. Hannah Talley shares the responsibility with Moss.

It's a deep-state job—not in a conspiratorial sense, but in its out-of-the-limelight nature and its reliance on knowledgeable, career professionals who keep the ballot honest and impartial. Observing how it works, I came to understand how this inconspicuous job brings order and trust to elections, by ensuring that candidates are legitimate, ballot issues are understandable, and election rules are diligently enforced.

Getting ballot information right is a challenge familiar to election managers everywhere. "People often think that everything just magically appears on the ballot," observed Jon Dolson, the election clerk for Sheboygan County, Wisconsin, when interviewed by the National Conference of State Legislatures a few years ago. "That is definitely not how it happens."

People get their names or community issues on the local ballot by filling out paperwork. And there is quite a lot of it, I learned at a seminar Moss and Talley held for city clerks representing most of St. Louis County's many municipalities, school districts, and other taxing entities. Each one manages filings in their bailiwick: mayors, treasurers, municipal judges, city attorneys, council members, trustees, or any of the other sometimes quirky municipal titles. The clerks deserve honorable mention as another unseen election force, not employed by the county election authority but essential to the process.

"It's a crazy job," said Chris Thomas, the city clerk of Hazelwood, Missouri, one of the county's larger municipalities. She's been doing this work for years, and it doesn't get any easier, she said. "But it comes with the territory. I don't see it as a burden, just a very busy time."

At the seminar, taking us deep into the election weeds, Talley handed out an inch-thick packet that included lists of state statutes pertaining to candidates, four pages of FAQs, a form for declaring one's candidacy and another for withdrawing, if candidates change their minds or realize they've filed for the wrong office—which they do. There's a deadline for that, too. Yet another form requires office-seekers to swear that they've paid their state taxes. There's even a companion form on which a whistleblower can file a complaint against a candidate believed to have failed to pay up.

Eric Fey, unobtrusively monitoring the proceedings from the back of the room, jumped in when the topic of throwing someone off the ballot arose during the session. "No one in this room can disqualify a candidate, just because someone says the candidate isn't legit in some way," he announced emphatically. "That's up to the legal system. This is the stuff that puts us in court every April, when someone objects to having their name removed from the election." Ask around, Fey told me later: Election directors do not like having to appear in court.

As the forms come in, Moss and Talley comb through them, enforcing deadlines, alerting clerks to mistakes, and juggling multiple rounds of editing and approvals. Ballot information isn't ready until Moss and Talley say it is.

"A lot of our job is to keep you and the candidates out of trouble," Moss explained to a crowd of very attentive veteran and rookie clerks, compulsively clicking pens and flipping back and forth through the lengthy syllabus. Some were refreshing their knowledge of a job they do for a few weeks once a year. Others were hearing the information for the first time and trying to keep up.

"There are a lot of ways to stumble," said Moss. I hadn't fully appreciated the scope of her knowledge or her been-there-done-that sense of humor until I saw her manage the two-hour tutorial. "For example, you can't use nicknames on our ballot," she said. "Once, we had a candidate who claimed that he went by the name 'Honest Abe.' Nope, not okay. Their ballot identification has to be an actual part of their name. We don't use doctor, reverend, sister, general, or nicknames like Doc or Coach."

That's not a universal prohibition. In Kansas, if you are known as "Farmer John," and you can get five residents of your county to attest under oath that it's your bona fide nickname, that's how it will appear on the ballot. Louisiana takes a wide-open, *laissez les bon temps rouler* view of ballot monikers. In 2019, "Phil Cowboy" Lemoine of New Orleans ran for state senate. Beldon "Noonie Man" Batiste, also from New Orleans, ran for the state house, and "Mike Chicken Commander" Boyter ran for sheriff in Caddo Parish. But one candidate for governor threatened to sue because the secretary of state's office suddenly took a hard line and refused to let him appear on the ballot as Gary "Go Gary" Landrieu, claiming that it wasn't a real nickname.

Sometimes, candidates go to extremes to stand out on the ballot. In 2014, in Arizona, after a failed attempt to get elected to Congress as a Republican, a candidate named Scott Fistler legally changed his name to one that he thought would make him more popular: Cesar Chavez. In Montgomery, Alabama, in 2010, to get around a prohibition on listing candidates as professor or doctor, a Republican candidate for governor, a retired physician, officially changed his first name to DR, as a marketing tool for his candidacy. Unfortunately for him, the state executive committee rejected his request to list his name that way on the primary ballot.

In St. Louis County, Moss and Talley are by necessity sticklers for everything: spelling, grammar, and punctuation in ballot propositions, and even pronunciation. For voters who need special assistance, St. Louis County—like many other jurisdictions—offers an audio ballot, an ADA-compliant feature of up-to-date voting systems. "We'll have someone with a beautiful voice say the candidates' names," explained Moss, "but they need to know how to pronounce them, and some aren't obvious."

So, one of the forms in the clerks' packets asks for guidance. On the left, the clerks list the candidate's name as it appears on the ballot. On the right, they give hints as to how to say it. Accompanying the form is a two-page key with standardized phonetic cues for filling in the "Pronounced As" column. One sample lists a candidate whose name is Tim Beauprez, offering the helpful phonetic pronunciation as "bo-PRAI." For the March 2020 election, St. Louis County selected the apparently multi-talented Beau Coker to fill the role of "the voice." "It was more about availability than talent," Coker said.

∎

This deep-background business of preparing information for a ballot is complicated. One especially tricky part is ballot order—the sequence in which candidates' names appear. Everyone covets the first spot.

There's good reason for that thinking. Research points to a "primacy effect": a natural tendency to choose the first answer when given many possibilities. Put another way, "options listed first are chosen more often than those that are not," and studies of elections bear out that notion. One study compared election results for two candidates for the Texas Supreme Court. They had the same last name—Green. The Green listed first won by nearly 20 percent. Many studies reveal less dramatic results—a top-of-the-ticket advantage more in the 2 to 8 percent range—but still significant, especially in multicandidate local contests, where razor-thin victories are familiar outcomes.

The scramble for first place can be contentious. Late in 2019, the Democratic National Committee filed lawsuits challenging ballot order rules in Georgia, Arizona, and Texas. Each has a Republican governor and a Republican-majority state legislature, and under those circumstances, those states' laws dictate that Republicans are listed first on statewide ballots. In those three states, some recent elections have been decided by a 1 or 2 percent margin. Given the primacy principle, Democrats contended that it would be fairer to rotate the ballot order by precinct or county, to avoid giving one party preferential treatment.

On the local level, the me-first impulse is the reason that candidates in so many jurisdictions literally camp out at election headquarters days or even weeks before the first day of filing. That is because, traditionally, first in line meant first on the ballot.

"Sometimes, we had tents outside for weeks," said Moss. Like concert-venue bouncers, office staff tracked the queue, on guard for line-jumpers, enforcing ad hoc rules on how long to hold someone's place when they went to lunch, and staying on top of who bailed out and lost their place, she said.

"It was crazy. A few times, someone who thought they had clout or who knew someone, would just come in and try to hang out in their buddy's office until filing opened and then jump the line," Moss said. That was before St. Louis County wised up and created a ballot-order lottery for countywide positions. Now, on the first day of filing, candidates draw random numbers to determine whose name goes first.

First-day queuing and pre-filing tent cities are still long-standing rituals in many jurisdictions. To tamp down the chaos, some have instituted lotteries and alphabetical randomization to determine ballot order. For candidates seeking statewide and legislative offices in Illinois, being in line at the secretary of state's office at 8 a.m., when filing opens, secures your place in a lottery to determine ballot position. Some Illinois candidates choose to wait until 4 p.m. because candidates in line at that hour go into a separate lottery for last place—a slot sometimes seen as an advantage, too. In California, on the eighty-second day before an election, the secretary of state conducts a randomized drawing of letters of the alphabet. The resulting order of letters becomes the "randomized alphabet" used to determine the order of candidates' names on the ballot.

▪

Surprisingly, candidates themselves are often very much in the dark about the mechanics of elections. They can consult the websites of secretaries of state for basics, like filing deadlines, financial regulations, and guidance on what it takes—fees, petitions, or both—to get on the ballot. Most, of necessity, catch on quickly to fundraising, hiring treasurers to handle the money and the required reporting. But first timers—particularly local municipal candidates—can be a bit thin on knowledge of their own districts and on absentee voting, voter registration, and other basic functions, and they don't have access to the sophisticated voter databases maintained by statewide and national parties. St. Louis County has a sub-department for that—Election Information Services (EIS). It used to be a bigger operation, but so much information has migrated to the secretary of state's website that EIS has been scaled back to a single desk.

Senior clerk Cliff Freebersyser is its sole proprietor. A quiet, unassuming gentleman assigned primarily to the absentee department, Freebersyser is also the answer man when candidates call with questions. He has worked in the election office for ten years. Although eligible for retirement, he said that he wanted to stick around for "just one more presidential"—a sentiment voiced by many long-term employees who thrive on the high-energy environment, value civic service, and just can't quite let go.

"Local candidates and elected officials ask for all kinds of things," said Freebersyser. "They want to know how many registered voters are in their district. Or recent voter turnout. But a lot of them don't even know what they don't know. I educate them on the information we can provide."

In Missouri, as in many other states, "any member of the public can request a list of registered voters and their voting history for a nominal fee," Eric Fey told me in an email.

"Missouri state law specifies exactly what information must be given to the public and by what means. Opposition research companies often submit requests for the voting and registration history of rival candidates." The law prohibits dissemination of Social Security numbers, phone numbers, and driver's license numbers. Nor are death records and court orders available to the public through EIS.

Some publicly available information can be embarrassing. "It always amuses me when we're asked to research the voting history of folks running for public office, and we find out that some haven't voted on a regular basis," said Fey.

Like many employees I observed and spoke with, Freebersyser does dual duty, helping other workers when his workflow ebbs and theirs approaches high tide. To get ahead of the looming 2020 surge, for example, the absentee department sent out letters to about fifty thousand people. In recent years, the targeted recipients had cast ballots using the curbside-voting option. The mailing asked if they wanted to try the more convenient alternative of voting absentee in the March 2020 presidential primary and/or the April municipal election. Also in the envelope was an invitation to join the twelve thousand people already enrolled on the jurisdiction's permanently disabled list, which would qualify them to receive absentee ballots automatically.

The phone began ringing as soon as that mailing hit, and I overheard Freebersyser patiently and repeatedly explaining the process one early December day. Less than thirty days later, the mailing had resulted in an increase of nearly five thousand enrollees on the permanently disabled list. No doubt, later in the cycle, Freebersyser would be toggling back to candidate inquiries and absentee-vote processing.

■

If the ability to switch gears, to pinch hit, and to see the interconnections among functions is a core element of cohesiveness and stability, Inessa Spring (pronunciation guide: "uh-NESS-uh") is its personification. Before she landed in election world, she worked for county government as an internal auditor—a job with far-reaching tentacles.

"When you're an internal auditor, you need to know different departments, do different things, so you have to learn what they do, and how they use things. You learn everything about everything, not in depth but enough to be able to analyze," she said. Four years ago, she applied for a job in elections. Her interviewer asked which department she thought she'd best fit into. "Give me the one with the most problems," she replied.

They did. She got information technology. "The communications between IT and everybody else was terrible," she told me. "Nobody was speaking the same language." Early on, she implemented an office-wide training program that raised the employees' competence in the applications they were using and freed up IT professionals to work on issues at a higher level than the repeated, basic questions about Outlook, Excel, and Word.

Others in the office noticed the resulting uptick in efficiency, and Spring quickly became a go-to person for reorganizing outdated procedures, streamlining processes, and adapting to new circumstances. A self-described neat freak and idea person, Spring comes from a background in which systematic thinking is a family trait: Her father is a coal-mine engineer, her mother is an explosives engineer, and her three daughters were all in engineering school when I interviewed her.

Spring's fingerprints are everywhere: in the warehouse, where her sharp eye factored significantly in the transport-cage packing routine; on the loading dock on election night, where she is the drill sergeant overseeing the critical turn-in of ballots and supplies; and in many other back-office areas, where trying out Plan A, refining it to Plan B, and eventually settling on Plan C is an Inessa Spring signature move.

"I just try to make things a little better," she told me. She gets the big picture, and she is an articulate spokesperson for the larger context and the need for everything and everyone to work together.

"Every department has their tasks. Somebody has to do the absentees, somebody has to build the elections, somebody has to get the polling places, somebody has to get the poll workers, somebody has to handle the equipment," said Spring. "If every department does their thing independently and successfully, then at the end all the pieces come together, and it becomes a successful election. Everybody here has skin in this game. It's so fast, and it's so critical, and you only have one shot. If you fail, you lose the trust of the community. It's literally all or nothing."

10

The Front Line

Poll worker Laura Wooten worked every election for seventy-nine years. In 2018, six months before she died at ninety-eight, she was assisting voters at her usual shift at the Lawrence Road firehouse in Lawrence, New Jersey. "Democracy is just a beautiful, beautiful thing," she said.

—NJ.com, March 31, 2019

DARYL BROWN'S COWORKERS REFER to him as "the hammer." He's sturdy. He's tall. He has a commanding presence, one that often prompts new acquaintances to ask him if he had a previous career in the military. (He didn't.) However, he doesn't look very threatening, and he's got a light-up-the-room smile. When he's not at election headquarters, he's an assistant pastor at A Sure Foundation Christian Church in nearby Florissant, Missouri. But if you're a problem-causing poll worker on election day, and you see him coming through the door of your precinct, you know you're in trouble. Like a classic teen-movie character—the middle-school vice-principal in charge of discipline—Brown is the person you're going to have to reckon with if you screw up.

Brown, though, is not the goon squad. Sit with him for a while, and you sense that if he's going to fire someone, he'll do it gently, respectfully, but undoubtedly firmly. That occasional role as enforcer is a natural outgrowth of his primary job: He's the department's trainer-in-chief. He not only knows the rules and proper procedures, he created some of them. He's the main brain behind an extensive training program designed to instill competence and confidence in poll workers—the frontline citizen bureaucrats who can make or break an election.

Brown views his work as a calling. "I'm in the people development business, at work and at church," he told me. "So, whether I'm trying to get them to improve their lives spiritually or be a better person, or 'Hey, be a good election judge,' it's the same thing. I'm trying to help people be the best that they can. I truly believe that if someone wants to learn, I can train them to do anything."

That's an admirable attitude because election training is a big responsibility with far-reaching consequences. In the anatomy of elections, poll workers can be the backbone or the Achilles' heel. Depending on where you vote, they may be called election officers, election judges, clerks, inspectors, or a range of other titles. But whatever the title, they are the public face of elections and often the only election official voters ever encounter. They can make the voting experience pleasant and rewarding. They can also make it difficult and miserable.

They have much in common with the people at your local motor-vehicle department. Their competence and attitudes are highly influential in how you view government in general, and elections specifically. There's much evidence of that phenomenon in American history. Not that long ago, states used poll workers to enforce discriminatory policies, to disenfranchise people of color in the South and immigrants in New York. That mistreatment generated justifiably negative views of government that continue to influence our political system today. As one University of Utah election researcher put it, "The people who apply the policy matter as much as the policy itself."

Poll workers take a lot of heat. If the lines are long, it's the poll workers' fault, goes the thinking, even if the real cause of delays is unexpectedly large voter turnout. If the machines are malfunctioning, it must be because poll workers don't know what they're doing. If you forgot your identification, and you're being told that you'll have to vote on a provisional ballot, the knee-jerk reaction is to blame the messenger. So, getting it right is imperative, but not as easy as voters might think.

Elections need poll workers like professional baseball needs umpires and a grounds crew. No one has devised a way to fully and securely automate voting—and with the national intelligence community sounding the alarm about potential electronic hacking, few people would want to. Even in states that have gone all-in on mail-in voting, human beings still run the show. If they are doing it right, poll workers are checks and balances, gatekeepers, educators, bulwarks against cheating, and de facto public-relations practitioners. Perhaps most critically, they are the front-line interpreters of election law: Often, they make the decision as to whether a person will be allowed to vote or not.

Most probably don't think of themselves in those conceptual terms. They're more focused on their practical responsibilities as early-morning door openers, voting machine setter-uppers, voter checker-inners, ballot issuers, rules explainers, guardians of the ballot box, and the end-of-day cleanup crew. And those are just the official duties. The training manual doesn't say anything about mopping up Big Gulp soft drinks spilled by voters, holding babies, performing CPR, or calling 911 when a voter faints or a coworker dies on the job. They cope with whatever comes along, sometimes doing heroic things, sometimes performing small human kindnesses. In Indiana in 2018, a team of poll workers trudged out to a snow-covered parking lot to help an 86-year-old voter find his treasured wedding ring, which had popped off onto the ground when he took off his gloves.

Nationwide, conducting elections requires an army of poll workers. In the 2018 EAC survey, forty-five states reported a total of more than 637,000 workers assisting at polling places during the November midterm elections. In terms of real armies, that's roughly equivalent to the combined 2018 active-duty rosters of the US Navy and the US Air Force.

Recruiting for the official armed forces isn't a slam dunk, but at least you can tantalize prospects with visions of traveling the world, getting an education, or having a decent-paying job that might translate into a post-military career. In contrast, for poll workers, the list of selling points boils down to one: being an engaged citizen doing a civic duty that makes a difference. That's a good reason, to be sure. But it's a tough sell. It's not easy to promote a job with ridiculously long hours—typically 5 or 6 a.m. to at least 7 p.m. when the polls close—and low pay—a national average of around $150 to $250 for the day, which covers the fourteen- to sixteen-hour shift plus, usually, an additional, mandatory multi-hour training session. So, it's not surprising that the 2018 EAC survey reported that two-thirds of election jurisdictions call poll-worker recruitment somewhat or very difficult.

"Pretty much, they have to do it because they care about it, or feel a passion for it, because it's not a lot of money to be sitting somewhere for sixteen hours," said Maureen Callahan, who works for St. Louis County as a poll-worker coordinator. Her job entails recruiting new poll workers, deploying them on election day, and keeping them happy so they'll come back. She says that in every election cycle, she needs to replace fifty or sixty people because they've moved, they're sick, they've lost interest, or they've died. "A lot of people understand and buy into the higher calling. They do it as a civic duty."

A woman I met at a training-review session embodies that attitude. Latricia Allen was preparing for her very first stint as a poll worker. She said she felt overwhelmed by her initial training class and was coming back to get it right. A former paralegal, Allen was finally fully recovered from a serious medical condition and ready to get back into civic activities. "I want to give back to my community," she said. "I want to be a good citizen. And I want to see some changes. I know that if you want to improve the situation, you have to do something about it yourself. I'm trying to walk the walk."

"But some do it just for the extra money," said Callahan. "A hundred-and-fifty bucks makes a big difference for a lot of people."

She's got that right, according to many administrators. Money is a key incentive. Questions about pay—how much and how soon—are often the first to come up in training sessions. "I've seen poll workers make mistakes on every kind of election day form," said Eric Fey. "But no one screws up their pay sheet."

Informal chats with St. Louis County poll workers I met at training classes confirm that view. Carol P. told me that the extra money supplements her regular pay as an Uber driver. Poll worker pay helps Linda W. make ends meet when her paycheck from a daycare center doesn't stretch quite far enough. "But it's not just the money," she added. "I like meeting the voters, interacting with new people, and feeling like I'm doing something important."

▪

There are qualifications to be a poll worker, but they're usually minimal and, of course, not uniform across the country. The bottom line in most states is: You need to be a registered voter, either in the state or in the local jurisdiction where you want to work; you need to take a short training course (but not necessarily pass an exam on the curriculum); and you need to speak, read, and write fluently in English—or know another language needed in the area. California's Orange County looks for workers who can provide language assistance in Chinese, Korean, Spanish, or Vietnamese at designated locations. Sonoma County, California, pays an extra $25 to bilingual poll workers who are fluent in English as well as Spanish, Tagalog, Vietnamese, or Khmer.

Some jurisdictions are quite specific about qualifications. They may require workers to have reliable transportation, have an email address and access to a computer and the internet, and/or be able to lift fifteen to thirty pounds. In many states, a person cannot be a candidate for public office or hold a public office while serving as a poll worker.

One odd employment policy popped up in news reports in 2015, when the board of elections in Hamilton County, Ohio, told 104 poll workers—who are "appointed" for a year, not officially "hired," one official told me—that they would not be invited back, after it was discovered that they had not voted in 2013 or 2014. "We want everyone to vote. If we have poll workers who don't vote, we're not encouraging that. They don't bother to vote and yet they work for the board of elections?" Tim Burke, chairman of the board reportedly said at the time. "We're not going to hire people who don't vote."

People do not voluntarily come out of the proverbial wood-work to apply for these jobs. Nebraska counters that reluctance by drafting its poll workers, jury-duty style. In other areas, recruitment requires a marketing strategy. In 2018, a new organization called All Voting Is Local launched what it called the nation's first multi-state effort to recruit poll workers. The project ran a national online campaign while also targeting Arizona, Florida, Ohio, Pennsylvania, and Wisconsin, with billboards and with ads in newspapers and on social media. One focus of the project is to help make the poll-worker population more reflective of the racial, ethnic, and age composition of the community it serves. Among the campaign's taglines is one that underscores the importance of fully staffing elections. Poll workers, it says, are "the difference between democracy and dysfunction." Organizers claim to have recruited more than three thousand poll workers in the targeted states.

Some jurisdictions are so strapped for election day personnel that they'll take almost anyone, some cynical observers have said. In an academic study published in 2005, researchers quoted an unnamed person in the California secretary of state's office as saying, "The counties only care about them—the poll workers—breathing. As long as they can do that and have a warm body, they're qualified."

That statement may be an exaggeration, but it's an indicator of how hard it can be to meet election-day manpower requirements. Solano County, California, is addressing this issue creatively, by offering service organizations, churches, and charity groups a financial incentive of $1,500 via its "Adopt-a-Poll" program. To earn the money, the organization takes on the job of supervising a designated polling place on election day and recruiting four to ten poll workers, depending on the needs of the location. The county provides materials and mandatory training, and it further rewards the organization with spiffy election day t-shirts for its workers and something that nonprofits often crave—official public recognition. As of early 2020, groups had adopted thirty of the county's nearly one hundred polling sites.

As a larger election jurisdiction, St. Louis County has the luxury of a deep bench of well-qualified, time-tested poll workers, developed over many years. But complacency is not an option, so they continue to recruit, constantly on the lookout for new ways to attract workers. One conventional approach is the old-school, "help wanted" sign. One is posted on the door to the election board, which shares a lobby with the county's high-traffic revenue department. They've also run ads on local radio stations. Another more recently invented tactic was to insert a plea for poll workers into the annual property-tax bills mailed out to all county homeowners. Another can't-ignore-it placement.

"That effort went very well," said Julie Leicht, who oversees the poll-worker operation as part of her deputy director job. "In 2018, we got five thousand responses." The same mailing in November 2019 had already yielded more than seven hundred inquiries just two weeks after it went out.

If it's so hard to get poll workers, why don't jurisdictions offer split shifts, to make the job more attractive, administrators are often asked. "I'm sure workers would love that," said Callahan.

"The problem is that we'd have to hire twice as many people, and we're already worried about just getting enough for one shift. It would also double the training load." The additional hurdles of maintaining continuity, plus potential second-shift no-shows, make a split-shift plan impractical. The nearly ubiquitous requirement to be able to tolerate a fourteen-hour shift is not going away any time soon.

■

The next step, keeping poll workers on board, is something of an art, as I learned during a lively group interview with six of the department's poll-worker coordinators. Fortunately for the team, a good percentage of people who try the job re-up, coming back year after year.

"I think I can say, without exaggeration, that we have some poll workers who have been with us for as many as fifty elections over the past ten years or so," said Daryl Brown. Department records indicate that at least one currently active poll worker—now in her 70s—has worked in 101 elections, so far. "A lot of people pride themselves on that longevity."

For those who need a bit more prodding, poll-worker managers have invented a variety of retention strategies, like seasonal newsletters and social media outreach. But they're often not nearly enough.

"Rapport is everything," said LaTasha Jackson. One of the newer members of the team, she arrived with essentially no knowledge of how elections work. Her previous job was as an office manager for a childcare facility. Working with toddlers and their sometimes-demanding parents gave her valuable experience in handling tricky situations that involve emotions, ego, and the need to play well with others, she said. That comment sparked an outburst of knowing guffaws from her coworkers around the conference table.

Like the other coordinators, she juggles a registry of between five hundred and six hundred names. "In between elections, I might send the poll workers on my list a personal text message. I keep notes in my files on vacations or surgeries or kids' weddings that they've mentioned, and I'll say, 'Hey, I'm just checking in, wanted to see how the wedding went,' stuff like that," she said. "With the size of the list I manage, I don't get to talk to everybody that many times, but I can make those little notes that mean something. I think it helps make a person feel valued, and when they feel appreciated, they're more likely to keep coming back."

Demographics play a role in recruitment and retention, too. Nationally, less than one-fifth of poll workers are younger than forty-one years old. More than two-thirds are over sixty-one.

Voters waiting in line at polling places sometimes can be overheard commenting on the advancing age of workers running the election. Their observations are correct. It's easier to recruit older workers because retirees don't have to give up a day of an upwardly mobile career to staff a position that may see little action in a low-turnout election.

Some jurisdictions report that it's getting harder every cycle to recruit poll workers, even in the older age groups that have traditionally been a mainstay of the election-day workforce. One reason behind this decline may be that, in an economy in which people are working multiple jobs to keep up, many have not accumulated very much in savings. They are postponing retirement, shrinking the pool of people available to work on election day.

The active roster of St. Louis County's 4,700 poll workers skews older, right in line with the national trend. At our group interview, the youngest and newest of the poll-worker coordinators, Matt Harms, exuberantly reeled off the numbers.

"Nineteen to 30 years old—158. Thirty to 40 years old—71. Forty-one to 50 years old—270. Ages 51 to 60—711," he said, proudly sharing his research. He came prepared and was clearly happy that I had asked about demographics. "Ages 61 to 70, we have 1,436 poll workers, the biggest group. But wait, there's more. We have 1,107 poll workers between the ages of 71 and 80, and 208 who are between 81 and 90—more in our oldest category than in our youngest. And there you have it. I rest my case."

■

Poll workers have a lot to learn. But before launching into the details of election-day procedures, it helps to start trainees off with a baseline understanding of the mission, the bigger picture in which they play a make-it-or-break-it role. In Indiana, the first line of the statewide poll worker's handbook states, "Your work on Election Day is not just another job but one that ensures the survival of our democracy. All across the state you are part of a massive effort that is making this great experiment we call America possible."

Another critical, and sometimes tricky, concept in training is the importance of equal treatment and respect. In Hanover, Massachusetts, "Respect for All Voters" is the heading for one section of the Election Workers Manual. "It is important that poll workers treat all voters with the same respect, courtesy and level of service, regardless of how they look, how they dress, or what language they speak," it says. "Voters of all backgrounds should be comfortably and respectfully able to participate in the voting process. All United States citizens, regardless of their proficiency in English, have the right to vote."

That, of course, is sage advice, not always internalized by workers, and sometimes overlooked in highly compressed training programs where rules rule, and where there's little time left over for philosophy.

The rules that typically get the most attention in training pertain to voter registration and identification. The rules differ from state to state, and in recent years, the laws have been in flux. Workers may have to relearn them from one election cycle to the next. In addition, poll workers need to understand procedures for voter sign-in; how to deal with people who show up at the wrong precinct; what on earth a provisional ballot is and when to use it; and many other rules that can trip them up, even if they are Rhodes scholars or simply dozed off in class for a few minutes.

Some top administrators are fluent in election-ese and can spout the statutes on demand because they've had years to absorb them. Poll workers, who do this job at most four times a year, must cram it all into their brains in a few hours and put what they've learned into play under public scrutiny on election day. Mistakes are inevitable. One election researcher put it this way: "Poll workers are like surgeons and distressed pilots— under pressure and with significant time constraints—but they have much less training in completing their tasks."

Many training programs fortify election workers with reference manuals and checklists to guide them through the morass. Some manuals, though, are as dense as a Russian novel and equally hard to follow, sometimes spanning as many as a hundred pages. On top of that, some jurisdictions expect poll workers to separately review both state and local guidelines. "No one, especially a temporary employee, can master all of that information and then apply it correctly in a high-pressure situation while voters are waiting," commented one researcher. "Election officials should not expect anyone, except the editor, to read the entire manual."

Training may also include some weight lifting, particularly in jurisdictions—St. Louis County among them—where poll workers set up voting equipment on election day. I participated as a trainee in a session at which poll workers practiced the election-day workout, which includes: unpacking the transport cage, placing folding tables in their upright and locked positions according to a site plan, doing a tricky ballot-box assembly, lugging the department's new thirty-pound printers to their designated locations, and hoisting them into position. Then, there was the step-by-step process of connecting cables to ports, firing up the equipment for a test run—and then reversing the entire sequence to simulate the end-of-day routine.

Our instructor told us it would take about twenty minutes to set up the equipment. Forty-five sweaty minutes later, most of the group had completed the job, some with ease, but some who were more tech-challenged needing handholding. (Some jurisdictions reportedly hire this process out, so that when poll workers arrive in the early morning hours of election day, it's all waiting for them. But there's considerable skepticism about the security of that scheme.)

To help make things go better, Daryl Brown instituted a program called Practice Makes Perfect (PMP), in which poll workers do a second go-round. Early in 2020, the department created a training video with a step-by-step walk-through of equipment setup, which poll workers can use as a refresher course, or even access on their poll pads on election day for guidance.

"For the new system, we're going to begin our training classes by saying, 'Forget everything you learned before, because we're going to be starting over,'" said Brown.

Training doesn't always stick, and neither do workers. "Five a.m." can be a trigger word for some new recruits. "That's why I make sure to introduce the required shift hours early in every session," said Brown. "You don't get up at 5 a.m., you have to be at work at 5. I've had people walk out as soon as I tell them that."

Others stay but bail out at the end of the session. "They come up to me after class and say, 'That's just too much information. I can't do this,'" said Brown.

Brown and his team of four trainers start scheduling classes six to eight weeks before every election. They try to limit class size to about twenty, so that they can connect with the trainees and observe whether they're catching on or going catatonic from information overload.

But keeping a low trainer-to-trainee ratio means running more sessions. In an election requiring three thousand poll workers, each trainer can expect to repeat the same instructions, answer the same questions, and demonstrate the identical equipment setup and break-down more than fifty times. Multiplying the number of sessions by the number of trainees, times four elections—coupled with the requirement that everybody must train or retrain for every election, Brown calculated that he and his team delivered their spiel to more than nineteen thousand trainees in 2018.

"You'd think it would get boring for us trainers, but it doesn't," said supervisor/trainer Haley Colter, who was a featured player in a series of training videos. "Every class is a little different, because the trainees bring their own experiences and their own viewpoints. Sometimes we learn from the poll workers. We're always reevaluating and tweaking."

With the changeover to new equipment, Colter had to learn an entirely new set of procedures in a very short time. Observing her at one of the first training sessions for the new system, I was impressed to see that she already knew the curriculum cold. Later in the cycle, I marveled at her ability to stay upbeat and not yawn as she delivered—for the umpteenth time—two packed hours of rules, procedures, and equipment-assembly instructions. Later, I ran into Colter as she was gathering materials for her final training session of the March/April 2020 cycle. She admitted that she was exhausted. Being a single mother raising a young daughter undoubtedly added to the stress. But she soldiered on. In one session, she rewarded people who posed what she rated as "particularly good questions" with a coveted prize—a plastic drinking cup emblazoned with the St. Louis County logo. It was a cheap incentive, but it apparently worked. After asking a question that she thought qualified for the prize, one trainee asked, "Do I get my cup now?"

■

Where poll workers put their training on the line depends partly on their preferences, partly on where they're needed, and partly on their party. The standard setup is eight poll workers per site, equally divided between the two major parties. But in some areas of St. Louis County, Republicans are an endangered species. In others, there's a scarcity of Democrats. That skew can mean that coordinators sometimes ask workers to deploy to areas farther away from home.

"Some people don't like to travel outside a 2.2–mile radius, that's what I'm finding out," said Matt Harms in the run-up to his first election as a coordinator. "I mean, they don't want to work at all if it's too far away. But most are pretty flexible." Some workers drive ten to fifteen miles to a polling site, if needed.

Some poll workers have staffed the same site for years—coordinators call them "default sites." They may have become friends and look forward to seeing one another—a compatibility factor that can smooth operations. Team members have been known to bring sandwiches, home-baked goods, and jugs of coffee to share with their coworkers-for-a-day. Occasionally, they go to extremes, laying out spreads worthy of a Christmas smorgasbord. Sometimes, though well-intentioned, they go too far.

"A few years ago, the buffets started getting out of hand, too elaborate and distracting, so we had to ask them to dial it back," said Christian Tolbert. One egregious example, he recalled, was during the 2008 presidential election, when a complaint about an extremely long line at one polling place prompted him to hop in his car with an associate to see what was up. "When we got there, the line was snaking around the block and not moving much at all. We discovered that the poll workers were having a barbecue. Even worse, they had failed to set up half of the voting machines, because they would have gotten in the way of the party."

Friendship and team spirit among poll workers generally are good things, but as in that 2008 barbecue brouhaha, they can have a downside, too. In a different, less intense election where turnout was low, a news crew arrived at a polling place and found the workers playing board games. "We were on national television, and our workers were playing Sorry," said Eric Fey. "After that, we started adding 'no board games' to our training presentations."

■

In addition to their prescribed duties, poll workers can be, informally, the eyes and ears of election administration. Among the many paper forms packed into polling-place materials, St. Louis County includes one called the poll-worker comment sheet. It's a blank piece of paper, coded to the polling location. Poll workers use them to record their overall observations, recommend procedural changes, describe problems they had with rules and policies, fess up to mistakes, and gripe about coworkers.

The comment sheets are public-record documents, so I checked out uncensored sets of them from some recent elections. A few came back just as they went out—pristine and blank, perhaps indicating that absolutely nothing remarkable happened, or perhaps that the workers were too swamped during the day and too wiped out at closing time to reflect on anything. Most, though, contained handwritten comments that offer an intriguing peek into a day in the life of a poll worker.

It must be heartwarming for recruiters and trainers to read the positive reports. "No issues" were the only two words on one sheet. "Great shift!" gushed another. "A great bunch of people to work with!" exclaimed a supervisor. One worker said it all by filling half the page with a large, hand-drawn smiley face and a bit of doggerel poetry: "Remember, remember/the 5th of November."

Other commenters had much more to say. Some filled both sides of the page with helpful suggestions for procedural changes, such as how to streamline the flow of voters and ideas for signs to guide voters along. They listed big problems, like long wait times on central-office telephone helplines or issues with poll pads or the database, and small issues, like running out of paper clips or staples. One suggested that administrators add antibacterial wipes to the supply package. A recurring thread was "we need a raise."

It can be hard out there for a poll worker. Throwing strangers together and placing them in a high-stress situation creates a perfect storm for misunderstandings and interpersonal problems. The comment sheets reflect that reality, too, and they hint at the kinds of behaviors that can result in a Daryl Brown intervention. "The supervisor has an attitude that is irritating to all the other workers. The other workers are threatening not to return," complained a coworker. "The assistant supervisor never returned from lunch," noted someone in a different polling place. "Don't make me work with Jennifer [not her real name] ever again," pleaded yet another.

The most memorable comment sheet I reviewed was an angry double-sided, almost minute-by-minute chronicle of one poll worker's job-shirking behavior. It read like a police stakeout: "5:01 am: Smoking in her car. 5:30 am: Smoking again. 6:25 am: Smoking again until 6:35 am. 7:05 am: Gone again! 8:49 to 8:55 am: Out. Excuse, she's getting a Pepsi. 9:10 am to 9:18 am: Out again! Excuse, she forgot her cheese/crackers! 86 minutes of breaks before lunch!"

Some commenters took the time to format their remarks in meticulously constructed bullet points. Others dashed theirs off in huge, hurried, it's-the-end-of-a-long-day, get-me-out-of-here letters. Taken together, and judging from the detailed information they include, the comment sheets paint a picture of a conscientious cadre of temporary workers who care about doing a good job in less-than-ideal circumstances—sometimes with less-than-ideal teammates.

After the election, Brown and the training team look at every comment sheet and follow up on problems. "We call anyone who didn't follow policy or procedures. We say, 'Hey, do you realize this is not what you learned in class?' We've learned that if you say, 'Next time you're working, please do it this way,' it usually sticks because we've made that personal contact, and they know someone is watching."

Some incidents are comical, like the worker who called 911 when the polling place ran out of toilet paper. Others are honest mistakes resulting from confusing election policies, gaps in training, or last-minute changes imposed by court decisions. In 2018, Missouri poll workers were caught in the crossfire of a battle over voter ID rules. The training manual said one thing, but a down-to-the-wire court ruling said another, causing widespread consternation at voter check-in tables, and prompting many calls to election-board hotlines.

Emphasizing that most poll workers do the right thing, and that on-the-job disagreements are almost never about politics, Leicht has nevertheless been on duty for some hair-on-fire incidents. Without naming names, she ticked off a few: people who show up drunk; workers who go rogue, intentionally deviating from the laws about voter ID, provisional voting, or eligibility because they disagree with them; the poll workers who got into a fist fight over who was supposed to do which job. "That's when we send in 'the hammer,'" said Leicht. "The message is 'your services are no longer required here.'"

■

For a special election in November 2019, I signed on as a poll worker. I helped staff a site where more than one thousand voters cast ballots in a steady stream that started with a line of people waiting at the door at 6 a.m. Veteran poll worker Barbara Stahl managed one of the new ballot-on-demand printers that was being road tested for the first time that day. She almost never sat down but seemed upbeat throughout the day. She didn't let on to voters how much her feet and back were aching from standing in one place hour after hour. Being a poll worker, she told me, is a highlight of her year.

"I love it," she said. "You feel a part of something big, and you get an inside look at how the system works. You meet a cross-section of people. It's an adrenaline rush. It doesn't hit you until the next day that you got up at 4 a.m. and worked sixteen hours."

Stahl's first shift as a poll worker was a trial by fire—the high-intensity 2008 presidential election. She showed up despite having walking pneumonia, and she has worked every presidential election since then, plus many other local elections in between. She doesn't do it for the money. She once used her poll-worker pay to splurge on a pair of designer shoes. She has made new friends, too: At the end of one election day, a coworker she'd just met at 5 a.m. took her to her home and gave her sprigs of berry bushes to plant in her garden. Somebody from the election board should probably make a promotional video about the joys of being a poll worker and cast Stahl in a starring role.

∎

Eric Fey compared the November 2019 debut of the new ballot-on-demand voting system to the "soft opening" of a new restaurant: no fanfare, a practice run to work out the kinks. It went well, but with only thirty polling places needed for the day, it wasn't a capacity-pushing stress test. The next big milestone would be the Missouri presidential primary in March 2020, when the full complement of polling places would be up and running, and poll workers would roll out an entirely new set of procedures. More than ever, those workers would be a critical cog in the election-day apparatus. It could all come down to their competence, their passion for the job, their willingness to adapt to change and, to a great extent, their stamina. The coordinators who recruited them, the trainers who schooled them, and the voters who rely on them would have a lot on the line.

Maureen Callahan knows the feeling. She summarized it in a single, poignant sentence. "Election day is my breathe-in-a-paper-bag moment."

11

Election Day. Live.

More than 270 election workers died in the ten days after Indonesia's April 2019 national elections. Health authorities blamed most of the deaths on fatigue-related illnesses caused by long hours spent counting millions of ballots by hand in sweltering conditions.
—*BBC World News, April 28, 2019*

3:45 A.M., TUESDAY, MARCH 10, 2020. Missouri presidential primary election day. Stephanie Hegger, the first staffer to arrive, unlocks the door and turns on the lights at St. Louis County election headquarters. Known for her high-energy persona and her intense dedication to the job, Hegger is a key member of the training team. Like election workers everywhere, she starts the big day with a pre-existing sleep deficit.

"I slept a few hours, I think," she tells me later in the day, showing no signs of slowing down. "My pre-election sleep routine is to wear myself out with work the day before, and then drop into bed as soon as I can." That's exactly what she did. The day before an election, she has a big critical job: assembling supply packets for technicians who will troubleshoot problems that crop up at polling places. Yesterday, it took all day and into the evening to gather and pack the materials and equipment designed to anticipate the anything-can-happen storyline of election day. By the time she finished, her fitness tracker had logged seventeen thousand steps.

4:00 A.M. Office workers have been arriving in a steady stream. Now, they're settling in, brewing the first pot of coffee, booting up spreadsheets, and readying themselves for what is about to hit them. Eric Fey, Rick Stream, Julie Leicht, and Christian Tolbert have done this many times, but today is different: It's the much-anticipated debut of the new voting system, and they need it to go smoothly. The polls will open in two hours.

The advance action begins in the department known as "judges," where the first order of business is for poll-worker coordinators to make sure that their polling places will be fully staffed. It's not looking good. By Monday night, more than one hundred poll workers had called in to cancel, citing fear of the looming coronavirus outbreak as their reason for staying home. There were so many calls that one staffer commandeered a whiteboard to create a coronavirus cancellation scorecard, decorating it with a cartoon rendering of a virus cell.

Election-day coronavirus no-shows are trending in primary elections across the country. Travis County, Texas, got off to a rocky Super Tuesday start on March 3 because so many election workers didn't report for duty as promised. The elections office had to fill in with their own staff and other employees, according to news reports. Similarly, in Yolo County, California, about 10 percent of poll workers backed out at the last minute on Super Tuesday, pointing to concerns about the virus. The county's chief elections official called the no-show rate double what is normal for an election and sent his team scrambling for replacements.

4:30 A.M. In St. Louis County, fifty more phone messages are already waiting, many of them announcing cancellations, but with no stated excuse. And the phones are still ringing. Poll workers are expected to be on the job at 5 a.m., to set up equipment and be ready for the first wave of voters at 6 a.m. It's thirty minutes until go-time. But these coordinators are well prepared for this contingency. Each has a backup list of at-home, fully trained standby workers who have agreed to be awake and dressed at 5 a.m., and ready to fill in if needed. An additional cadre of forty or so standbys is beginning to gather in a nearby training room to await deployment. The coordinators won't know exactly how many replacements they're going to need, where they'll need them, or how many Republicans or Democrats will be required until they hear from poll managers in the field.

4:45 A.M. The election-day army of three thousand poll workers is fanning out across the county, heading for their assignments at the 357 polling places activated for this election. "The name of the game in the early morning is staffing," says deputy director Julie Leicht, who has arrived in a festive red, election-day pantsuit. "The judges department will be crazy until 7 a.m. Until then, we're sort of improvising."

5:00 A.M. All eyes in the judges department are on an oversized computer monitor, which uses data from poll pads to track polling place openings and worker sign-ins. Coordinators are donning headsets, breaking out their backup lists, opening Google maps on their screens, and steeling themselves for the inevitable pre-dawn rush of lost poll workers and no-shows. They don't have to wait long. The "deedle-deedle" electronic ring tone goes viral in the first five minutes, and everyone is fielding calls non-stop on a phone queue dedicated to the needs of distressed poll workers.

Disoriented workers in search of their assigned locations constitute a large percentage of the callers. "Where are you now? What do you see?" Leigh Ann Warrington asks a caller. She's looking at an aerial view of Washington University, where the worker is wandering around in the dark. She offers turn-by-turn walking directions, until the worker says that she has found the fieldhouse that contains her polling place. She tells Warrington that she can see lights inside but can't find the door. Warrington guides her along the perimeter of the building, until the caller says she sees her destination. "Bang on the window. Yell. Whatever it takes," advises Warrington. After almost fifteen minutes on the phone, she has resolved that situation. As soon as she disconnects, another call comes in.

5:40 A.M. The tracking software indicates that 63 percent of poll workers have signed in. This is a late start. Matt Harms is talking to a worker who can't find the entrance to his polling place at Jennings Senior High School. "He's been driving around for thirty minutes," says Harms, clearly exasperated, but not revealing his frustration to the caller. Harms has run out of ways to describe where to go. He puts the caller on hold, contacts a polling-place manager inside the school, and asks him to go outside to flag down the worker. Harms is also dealing with no-shows, tracking who is missing and calling workers to see if they're on the way. "It's a never-ending story," he says later in the day, when things have calmed down. "The first hour and a half is a real gut-getter."

"The thing is, most of the workers really care about the job, and they regret not being able to work on election day," says Cindy Carberry, a longtime veteran of the judges department. She has just gotten off the line with a worker who sounded very ill and was reporting that she had a 102-degree fever. "She told me, 'If you need me, I can wear a mask and come in.'"

Simultaneously, one department over, the mapping guys are responding to their own early-morning issues: locked doors, lost keys, poorly marked or blocked entrances. "Everything under the sun becomes a problem on election day," says Rob Ryan. "Not enough tables and chairs. It's too hot or too cold in the polling place. A school has made bathrooms inaccessible to poll workers. We're in charge of solving all these problems and more."

The biggest facility emergency occurred yesterday. During a meeting of the department's top administrators, Ryan burst in with a surprise announcement. "This isn't going to be good, boss," he said. "Friendship Village just called in to say that they don't want to be a polling place tomorrow because of coronavirus."

The precinct assigned to Friendship Village—a senior citizens' facility—includes about two thousand registered voters, many of whom live at the center. Eric Fey called the administrator, trying to explain the logistical problems that the last-minute change would create, and pleaded for the facility to stay on board. It didn't work. Ryan sprang into action, finding a new location nearby. The warehouse dispatched a truck to relocate the equipment that had already been delivered. But they still had to figure out a way to notify voters of the sudden change of venue. Someone called someone in county government and got them to loan the election board two outdoor electronic message boards to get the word out. Later, Ryan went out to the old site to post signs about the location change.

Losing a polling place on election day is the wranglers' nightmare. But as annoying as the Friendship Village ghosting was, it wasn't nearly as bad as what happened in Nashville, Tennessee, one week earlier. A cluster of tornados roared through town in the early morning of Super Tuesday, killing at least two dozen people. In the aftermath, with trees and power poles blocking streets and with many buildings sustaining significant damage, Davidson County election administrators had to hurriedly shift voters from more than twenty polling places to alternative sites.

6:00 A.M. Lift-off in St. Louis County. Polls are opening. Early voters are already lined up at the doors of some polling places. Almost immediately, there are signs of trouble. The election office itself is a polling place. With the very first voter, the poll workers staffing it have hit a snag. The process is supposed to work like this: After showing proper identification, the voter signs in on the poll pad—an iPad that a commercial software company has programmed to replace the cumbersome, manual poll books used for many years. The poll pad recognizes the voter and instructs a small printer to generate a voter ticket. In turn, another poll worker inserts the personalized ticket into a ballot printer, which churns out the voter's ballot.

This morning, that's not happening. Somehow, the poll pad isn't synching with the ticket printer. But you can't vote without a ticket. System down. The poll workers remember their training: They unplug the ticket printer and reconnect it to the poll pad. They reboot the poll pad. Nothing works. Voters are waiting, noticing, drumming their fingers impatiently. Inessa Spring, an IT guru who knows just about everything about poll pads and ticket printers, tries to help. "We've been using poll pads since 2017, and we've never had this problem," she says, her systems-manager brain in overdrive as she tries to figure out what is wrong. It's not the new ballot-on-demand system that's malfunctioning, it's something that has been in use and trouble free for more than three years.

In the nearby command center, the technical-support line begins to blow up with calls. The same check-in problem is plaguing polling places countywide.

6:10 A.M. The good news is that there's a backup plan. Among the supplies issued to every polling place, St. Louis County election planners wisely included packets of old-school, manual voting tickets that will let poll workers bypass the malfunctioning ticket printers and allow voters to do what they came for. The word comes down: "Break out the manual voting tickets until we figure out the problem." Beau Coker, recently promoted to information technology, sends a countywide alert to poll workers.

6:25 A.M. The bad news is that some poll workers are panicking. Training classes covered the procedures for issuing manual voting tickets, but under the pressure of election day, it's easy to forget a topic that took up just a few minutes of a three-and-a-half-hour session. The training staff manning the tech line are walking workers through the low-tech work-around. Coker is jawboning the company that programs the poll pads. They reassure him that it's all just a software-programming foul-up that they can easily fix. Tech-line staffers start giving poll workers instructions on how to do a "hard reset" of poll pads to solve the problem. Inessa Spring whips up a step-by-step instruction sheet and passes copies around the command center.

6:35 A.M. Back in the judges department, the staffing scramble continues. Matt Harms has compiled a list of shortages, and coordinators are activating their at-home standbys, making sure that they fill the slots with the required balance of Democrats and Republicans.

6:56 A.M. A call from a local television news department prompts Hannah Talley to jump out of her chair in the command center and track down Eric Fey. "They're getting calls saying that voters are being turned away because the equipment isn't working," she tells him. It's the first of a rash of similar calls that will keep Fey and Stream busy dousing media fires for the rest of the day. Turning voters away is a cardinal sin in elections, and St. Louis County's training program emphasizes that poll workers should do everything in their power to enable voters to cast ballots. "You just don't turn away voters," Rick Stream asserts. Conversations on the tech-support line reflect that bedrock philosophy. "Keep him there until we work this out," I hear one staffer say. "Do not tell her she can't vote," says another.

Historically, of course, many voters across the country have found themselves rejected on election day, often for malicious reasons. If there were turn-aways in St. Louis County today, it's probably safe to say that they occurred because of poll-worker panic or flat-out errors. That's what happens in Kansas City, when the city's mayor, Quinton Lucas, is told he can't vote because the poll worker cannot find him in the voter database. He has proper identification. He knows he's a registered voter. But he leaves the polling place without casting a ballot. Later, a supervisor discovers that the poll worker had erroneously entered the mayor's first name as his last name. They contact him, and he returns to vote.

7:30 A.M. In the ready room, standbys awaiting their assignments scroll through social media, sip coffee, read books, and review training manuals. Mark Dana, who retired a few years ago from Boeing's human resources department, says he'll go anywhere they send him. He's an avid bicyclist who has wheeled his way around most of St. Louis County, so he knows the territory. "I don't do this for the money," he says. "I just genuinely believe in the democratic process and in doing what I can to ensure that people can vote."

I start to talk with another waiting worker, who is doing standby duty for the first time. But just as we begin to chat, a poll-worker coordinator whooshes in and summons all Republicans to the front of the room to get their assignments. She tells me that thirty to forty minutes from now, every standby will have been deployed. The worker I tried to interview is going to an elementary school in an area of the county she's never visited before, but on her way out the door, she tells me she's game for the challenge. Earlier, Julie Leicht told me that the department eventually offers every standby a slot, even if all polling places are fully staffed, as a way of honoring their early-morning effort and giving them a chance to help out.

7:45 A.M. To someone who's not answering the tech-support hotline, chasing down AWOL workers, or fielding media calls, the vibe seems calmer. I quickly realize, however, that my perception of the situation is an illusion. While poll workers seem to be adapting to the manual voter ticket workaround, there are new poll pad problems. Inessa Spring explains the current thinking to me: When the software vendor attempted to push out the "easy fix" it was touting, sending it to twelve hundred poll pads all at once may have overloaded the bandwidth of the communications network that handles the election department's traffic. And it's not just any network. It's a special cellular pipeline—not an internet connection—that keeps election information separate, and therefore secure, from general users. They thought they had that covered. Now, a large percentage of the poll pads aren't communicating with headquarters. Not only didn't they get the fix, they're not getting recent updates on changes of addresses, name changes, and other essential voter information. Fortunately, at every polling place, there's one poll pad that is specially programmed as the "solutions desk," and those are working.

Surprisingly, the problems that administrators were most worried about—issues with the new ballot-on-demand printers or glitches in the new scanners—are not in the mix at all. A week ago, Fey led a worst-case-scenario exercise, where his team gamed out high-risk possibilities. They talked about the fully equipped, off-site, emergency tabulation center that could be activated if an area-wide power outage crippled their normal site. They had special battery-powered generators, preloaded on technicians' trucks, to be delivered if a localized power outage took down a polling place. They even held a tornado drill for the entire office a few days before the election. But a bandwidth problem? Not on the radar. As Fey has said many times, "In every election, something happens that you could never have imagined."

Last week, as Fey's team walked through simulated disasters, Los Angeles County, California, was experiencing a real-world, epic election-day meltdown on all-important Super Tuesday. The largest election jurisdiction in the country was rolling out three new election elements at once: a $300 million custom ballot-marking system that had been in development for ten years; a new configuration that eliminated more than 4,000 neighborhood polling places and replaced them with 960 strategically located vote centers; and an early-voting option. Apparently, it was too much, too soon. Voters waited in line for three hours or more. People couldn't find their vote centers. About one-fifth of the new machines did not work properly and had to be replaced. Not as many people voted early as had been estimated, creating an unexpected election-day crush.

Dean Logan, LA County's registrar of voters, had to do the election director's walk of shame. "Obviously, this was not the rollout we had hoped for. A lot of that falls on my shoulders," he said in a high-profile apology. He and his staff are now laser-focused on working out the kinks before the ultra-high-stakes November 2020 presidential election. Secretly, some longtime LA County administrators and voters may be longing for simpler times, when the county voted using a system known as "InkaVote." In that now-quaint system, voters used an ink stamper to fill in the bubbles printed on their ballots.

As election-day problems go, the ones facing Fey and Logan are serious, but perhaps not as terrifying as something that happened during India's national election in 2019. According to news reports, in one polling place in the southern state of

Kerala, panic spread when voters and officials realized that there was a snake stuck in an electronic voting machine. Voting stopped for two hours while a brave election official wrestled it out.

8:25 A.M. The tech support line is on overload. Two and a half hours after the polls opened, help-line staffer Cassie Klosterman is instructing a poll worker on the basics of how her polling place should have been set up. Stephanie Hegger is remotely holding a worker's hand as he struggles to understand the manual voter-ticket routine, which, she reminds him gently, until the introduction of poll pads had been a part of voter check-in for years. As she completes the call, she announces that she's taking her first break of the day, a mad rush to the restroom.

The "command center," where the tech line lives, is a fancy name for a group of tables arranged in a rectangle in an open space near the directors' offices. It's equipped with laptops and phones for ten workers. A tangle of cables and power strips snakes between workstations and under the tables. Along one wall, three large monitors display data from a program called the Centralized Election Management System: a running tally of incoming phone calls; the number of calls waiting; a graph showing voter turnout, hour by hour (at 8:40 a.m., it's 7 percent); a list of problem tickets generated by calls ("irate voter," "voter in wrong location," "printer not working," and, of course, "poll pad not synching"). Manning the phones are trainers and full-time staffers with impressive, nearly encyclopedic knowledge of the rules, processes, and granular details that poll workers are contending with out in the field. When they're not sure, they consult with one another, or they flip through the 124-page poll workers' training manual. Periodically, Fey, Stream, Leicht, or Tolbert hovers at the command center, observing the action and providing critical updates to the staffers, who are pinned down by the unending queue of calls.

"When we hear what the support staff is dealing with on the phones, we are in awe that everything works as well as it does," says Leicht.

9:00 A.M. Two election board commissioners arrive at the office to observe the real-world operations of the organization they oversee from on high. Fey and Stream bring them up to speed on the problems they're working to overcome today. A television news reporter shows up, wanting an interview about the polling-place issues. Fey obliges. Board chairman Sharon Buchanan-McClure observes the interview and volunteers to help with additional media inquiries that are surely in the works. For their national coverage of this presidential primary election day, news giant CNN has chosen a polling place in Webster Groves, a municipality in St. Louis County, as its Missouri outpost. Buchanan-McClure arranges to represent the board as an interviewee. She'll be good. She knows her stuff. She's articulate, and she has an authoritative voice.

In her role as a board member, Peggy Barnhart is observing, too. Watching the tech-support staffers as they handle whatever comes their way, she says, "There's just something about elections that brings out the best in people." Rick Stream, standing next to her, jokingly adds a coda to her words. "Mostly," he says.

9:45 A.M. Walking along the open corridor next to the judges department, I hear one side of a phone conversation. "No, ma'am, we don't supply gloves, but we have hand sanitizer at every polling place," says a temp worker to a voter concerned about coronavirus.

The command center is not the only telephone hot spot this morning. Using a setup considered by election experts as a best practice, in addition to the main, publicly published phone number, the department has established separate phone lines for specific types of issues: questions from voters; questions for poll-worker coordinators; absentee information; facilities issues; technical problems; injuries to poll workers or voters. They are listed prominently on page one of the poll workers' training manual. They're all ringing. No matter their normal job description, everyone here is a troubleshooter on election day.

The issue du jour is voter registration. Many of the poll pads have still not been able to receive updates, so voters who may have moved or changed their names in the past month are not turning up in the database with the correct information. That problem hits hard at polling-place check-in tables, and poll workers are calling in droves. Fortunately, workers at headquarters have access to the latest information in the statewide Missouri Consolidated Voter Registration database (MCVR). When a poll worker calls in, staffers enter the voter's name into MCVR and try to confirm that they're registered. "He's a good voter. I see him in the database. He can vote," I hear Matt Harms say, after finding one listing. Not all calls go that smoothly, though. Nearby, a temporary worker named Gwen tells me that she has had some rather tense calls. "It's okay. I can handle it," she says. "I just go back to my old social-work days, and I calm them down."

10:11 A.M. Human resources chief Amy Blankenship circulates through the office, announcing the arrival of brunch in the break room. It's a catered affair, a hearty smorgasbord with bacon, scrambled eggs, ham, potatoes, biscuits, and fruit platters. Almost everyone eventually migrates in. Too busy to sit down at a lunch table, they load up plates and take them back to their desks. There will be another round of catering at dinner time.

As she watches to make sure that the buffet is running smoothly, Blankenship tells me about something scary that happened this morning. One of the department's technicians had a heart attack outside a polling place. Noticing that he was stumbling around in the parking lot, voters called 911, and he was transported to a nearby hospital.

A few minutes later, I learn that there's been an incident in nearby St. Louis City, where news reports say that a person—possibly a voter—intentionally backed his car into the polling place at a church, threatened workers, and threw a liquid—water or perhaps bleach—at them. Police officers took him to a hospital in handcuffs. The city board of elections closed the polling place and quickly found a substitute location.

10:45 A.M. Matt Chellis and Pat Stinnett, two temporary workers, are sitting at a table near the employee entrance at the front of election headquarters, waiting for instructions. They are on call for unexpected contingencies. Each has a blue duffel bag containing items that might need to be delivered to a polling place in a pinch: pens, extra administrative forms, note pads, manual voter tickets, extra "I Voted" stickers, yellow envelopes for provisional ballots, and even blue painter's tape, a tape measure, and a piece of chalk, for use if someone needs to mark off the twenty-five-foot limit for electioneering near a polling place. They are not very busy today, but they're standing by, Chellis tells me, because "we're here to help keep the election safe." Just then, Rob Ryan puts Chellis to work, handing him three directional signs to deliver to a polling place that voters are struggling to locate.

Now that the early-morning staffing scramble has subsided, poll-worker coordinators have some breathing room. Between answering voter registration calls, they're updating their lists and chatting with their cohorts about how the morning has gone. LaTasha Jackson is spot-calling some of her first-time poll workers, to see how it's going. "I'm just checking in," she says. "I get some who say it's not so great, but I get more who find that they like working the polls a lot."

It has been an intense morning, but it's not all bad. "When you're cooped up in the office, all you see are the problems," Fey tells me. "It's a scramble. Everything comes at you fast and furious. But you don't have all the information." To get some perspective from the outside world, Fey texts his wife, asking her to tell him how things are going at their neighborhood polling place. They told her there were no problems at all, she reports.

11:30 A.M. Everybody working on election day has exercised their legitimate option to vote absentee. I'm curious about how things are going at polling places beyond the high-intensity headquarters bubble, so I've waited until election day to vote live at my neighborhood location. I drive to the church recently designated as my polling place, replacing the school library where I've voted for years. A few cars dot the parking lot. Only one other voter is in the room when I enter. There's a bottle of hand sanitizer on the check-in table. I recognize one of the poll workers as the parent of one of my children's friends, and we say hello. But we do not shake hands.

Everything goes according to plan. The poll pad recognizes me and prints my voter ticket. A poll worker inserts my ticket into the ballot printer, and out comes my ballot. The Democrat and Republican initial the ballot as prescribed and hand it to me. I ask if they have had problems with poll pads today, and they say no. Based on my observations today, I mentally count them among the lucky ones. I take my ballot to a table and pause before picking up the black pen provided by the polling place, thinking about germs, and happy that there's hand sanitizer to apply after I vote. I fill in the rectangle. I walk to the scanner and feed my ballot into the slot with the flashing green arrows. After a few seconds, an American flag appears on the screen, signaling that my vote has been recorded.

It's easy, deceptively so, because today, as never before, I'm acutely aware of how much effort has gone on behind the scenes to make this simple act of democracy possible.

1:30 P.M. Headquarters is still humming. Stream and Fey have been doing interviews all day, trying to emphasize the positives and feeling, it appears, that reporters are making the situation sound worse than it really is.

Rob Ryan reports a power outage at the Chinese Christian Gospel Church, caused when a car hit a nearby power box. They are ready for this. It's an opportunity to field-test the heavy-duty, battery-powered generators they purchased several months ago. The generators can run the equipment in a single polling place for an entire day. They became a necessity when St. Louis County adopted the new ballot-on-demand configuration. The old touchscreen machines had built-in battery backup. But the new system uses off-the-shelf printers, which do not come similarly equipped and draw more amperage than a home-office battery backup can provide. With no preprinted ballots to rely on, a power outage could halt voting at a polling place. Christian Tolbert tells me that department shoppers found the generators at Home Depot and bought seven of them. Tolbert has a sense of pride about them because they are an innovative solution. He tells me, "We showed them to the people at Hart InterCivic, who sold us the ballot-on-demand system, and they said, 'Wow! Where'd you get those?'"

2:30 P.M. Calls to the tech-support line have slowed only slightly. Stephanie Hegger explains to a voter who is seventeen and a half that, although he's eligible to be registered now, he can't vote until he's eighteen years old.

Hanna Talley talks to a man who has shown up to vote, but whose record in the database indicates that he has already voted absentee. He insists that he didn't and that if the database shows that he voted, it must have been someone impersonating him. In fact, Talley tells him, the record shows that he voted absentee in person at one of the county's satellite polling places, so it couldn't have been anyone else.

Cassie Klosterman tries to help a poll worker deal with a voter who doesn't want to do what the rules dictate for the presidential-preference primary—select the ballot from one party. In this election, voters can choose among ballots issued by the Republican, Democratic, Libertarian, Constitution, or

Green parties. The operative word is "or." This voter doesn't like the rules, says Klosterman. "He says he wants to vote on all of them."

The calls are not all complaints and problems. Klosterman, the twenty-something staffer who manages the department's social-media accounts, reads aloud a tweet that has come across her feed. "I just want to thank the poll workers at my polling place. Voting was quick and easy, and they were very polite," it says. Not long after that, trainer-in-chief Daryl Brown, who has been on the tech-support line most of the day, receives a text message from a poll worker. "I wanted to let you know that everything is good. There's no stress today." Eric Fey, who has just meandered over to the command center for the umpteenth time, hears that and exclaims, "Bless her heart!"

After more than nine hours of nonstop, stressful trouble-shooting, it must be a gratifying moment. Unfortunately, election workers everywhere face the harsh reality that they'll get very few pats on the back for doing a good job.

3:00 P.M. During a lull in call volume, as staffers chat, the subject of making election day a holiday comes up. Someone mentions that Sandusky, Ohio, is among the first cities in the United States to declare election day a day off for municipal employees. Some voting-rights activists have called for celebrating Martin Luther King Day on election day in November to honor his work and to make national elections a federal holiday. Others have pushed for eliminating Columbus Day and swapping it out for election day.

Cassie Klosterman, who has a degree in political science, has strong opinions on the subject, and she rattles off an impressive, impromptu two-minute seminar on the pros and cons—mostly the cons. Many people in the world of election services do not support making election day a holiday, she says. "First, it sends a message that elections happen only once a year, and that national elections are the only ones that count," she begins. "Also, when you let city employees take the day off, you're limiting public transportation, which can make it harder for some people to get to the polls, especially lower-income voters. A better solution would be to make election day not the only day you can vote but, instead, the last day you can vote."

4:30 P.M. With two and a half hours to go until polls close, I look for signs of an office-wide adrenaline crash, but nobody is visibly slowing down. Daryl Brown, momentarily slumping in his chair and rubbing his eyes, springs back into action quickly when the next call in the queue lights up his phone console.

Reporters from two local television stations are setting up for live shots for the 5 p.m. and 6 p.m. newscasts. Board member Peggy Barnhart, whose professional background is in communications, works with the reporters to help them get the story straight. During the broadcast, she cringes as one reporter posts a list of polling places where voters have allegedly been turned away.

6:20 P.M. Eric Fey is sitting at his office desk, swapping out his dress shoes for his election-night sneakers. It's a tradition, he says. He needs comfortable shoes for his job as "runner" when ballots start coming in about an hour from now. Also, he is the "sneaker net," the term he uses for the way he transfers ballot tallies from the tabulation room to the computer that uploads the results to the department's website—not via an internet connection, but by walking a secure thumb drive from point to point.

7:00 P.M. Polls officially close, except for people already standing in line. There are few of these, as the command center's monitors show a total turnout rate of 31 percent, a below-average figure. The tech line gets a call from a polling place announcing that they have already packed up their equipment and are ready to go home, a bit early in the view of the training team. A few after-hours calls come in, with questions about procedures for shutting down the equipment. Overall, the office buzz has died down, and the phones are quiet.

But election day is not over. While temporary workers are dismissed, none of the full-time staff is going home yet. There is still a lot to accomplish. The workers manning the on-site polling place get out their closing checklist and begin shutting down the equipment, mirroring what is happening at the other 356 sites across the county. Poll-worker coordinators and mapping guys congratulate one another for overcoming the challenges they faced today and start swapping stories. On-call workers Stinnett and Chellis are still at their post, in case there's a last-minute need for drivers to transport materials back to the office.

7:15 P.M. The action shifts to the warehouse and the tabulation room. Members of the turn-in team have grabbed their sweaters and coats and have migrated to the warehouse for the final act of the election show. One loading-bay door is open, and it's chilly out there.

Julie Leicht is taking informal bets on when the first turn-in will arrive. It's anybody's guess because this is the first time the full complement of poll workers in the field has closed down and packed up the new system.

To ensure the security of the election, turn-in must be airtight. Two items are most critical: the electronic flash drives that have been locked into the scanners all day, recording the votes from the paper ballots; and the paper ballots themselves, which are the fail-safe backup. St. Louis County requires a Democrat and a Republican to ride together as flash drives and ballots are returned to headquarters. Some turn-in teams get police escorts. For efficiency, they've created centralized drop-off points, so that 357 cars don't have to drive to the warehouse. Two or three cars wait at each drop-off location. When the first car reaches its capacity, it takes off. The second waits for the next load, ensuring a continuous flow and preventing delays because of problems at a few polling locations. In traffic-clogged, sprawling Los Angeles County, by comparison, some turn-ins come via helicopter.

In the warehouse, the ubiquitous Inessa Spring has organized a military-grade system for logging in, sorting, and shelving the election-day materials that turn-in deputies are about to bring back. Her twelve team members are the same trusted full-timers who since 5 a.m. have been answering phones, calling poll workers, and troubleshooting the issues of the day. As they seat themselves at a long row of tables, Spring explains the designated job for each station. They'll be processing what has come to be known over decades as "the orange pouch," a flat, rectangular canvas bag with assorted clear-plastic compartments, pockets, and zippers. Before every election, workers load the most critical supplies into four hundred of them—one for every potential polling place—in a precisely prescribed, uniform configuration.

The orange pouch is a big deal and has been for many years. Losing track of even one is a major foul-up in election security, as the late Dick Bauer, a former assistant director, learned in the 1990s. Acting as a turn-in deputy one election night, he arrived at election headquarters and saw that he did not have the orange pouch. In a heart-thumping moment, he realized that he had left it on the roof of his car, and that it had undoubtedly fallen off as he drove. Frantically, he retraced his route, scouring the road for the missing pouch. Then he saw a street-sweeping truck. He flagged down the driver and asked him if he had, perhaps, swept up the bag. The driver looked in the bin, and there it was—flattened, chewed up, and caked with street dirt. Eric Fey has kept it in his office ever since.

Tonight, job one regarding the orange pouch is to remove the flash drive from a special compartment, which has been sealed for security at the polling place, and then scan its unique identifying code. The drive then will go into a plastic bin at the head of the table, where it is closely guarded. When a few drives have accumulated in the bin, a runner will take them to the tabulation room. Farther down the disassembly line, team members will log in smartphones and charging cables and sort other items into bins arranged on a shelving system at the end of the line.

"The chain of custody of ballots is critical," says Sam Derheimer, director of government affairs for Hart InterCivic, as he observes the process. "These folks have got this figured out. It's an extremely well-organized system. They're among the best that I've seen."

7:38 P.M. The first car arrives. The warehouse crew has created a one-way, drop-off lane indicated by orange traffic cones, which the driver dutifully enters. Three workers greet the driver and grab the all-important orange pouch and the duffel containing the paper ballots. They place them on a conveyor belt that warehouse supervisor Craig Hite has rented and send them up the ramp. Up top, a worker scans the bar code on the duffel. Workers transfer the ballot bags to a matrix of metal shelves labeled for each precinct. The orange pouch goes to Spring's assembly line.

8:30 P.M. The process is in full swing, with cars lining up in the drop-off lane. Some of them have duffels and orange pouches from more than a dozen polling locations. A large monitor tracking the scan-ins indicates that 20 percent of precincts are in. But the pace is speeding up. There is no downtime on the assembly line. Frontline office worker Melissa Moore is limping with knee pain as she sorts paperwork from an orange pouch. "After thirty-six years in the office, I think I'm getting too old for this," she says. But she sticks with it.

9:00 P.M. Flash drives have been arriving in the tabulation room in batches, and the top-level team inside is checking them in and processing them nonstop. They're using the new Hart tabulation system for the first time in a full election, and there are no surprises. There shouldn't be. Several weeks ago, they performed logic and accuracy testing, which is required by law before every election, to make sure that the scanners and the tabulating machines yield true results. Last Thursday, they did a similar public test, which was attended by only one person from the public: me. They showed me the results. It all checked out.

No one gets into the tab room without special identification. That's standard operating procedure, or should be, in most jurisdictions. Here, to open the door, a Republican and a Democrat must swipe their electronically coded keycards simultaneously. In Cuyahoga County, Ohio, where opening the tab-room door requires a numeric code, a member of one party has the first half of the code, while a member of the other party has the second half.

A young woman from Edison Research and a reporter from the Associated Press sit in the hallway, waiting to send results, as they become public, to their organizations. The more than ten thousand absentee ballots received by the deadline were tabulated earlier in the day, and they were posted by about 7:15 p.m. Eric Fey, striding down the hall in his spiffy new sneakers, walks a set of preliminary, unofficial returns to the front office, where they'll be released to the press, posted on the department's website, and reported to the Missouri secretary of state.

9:40 P.M. Cheers and applause in the warehouse, as the last orange pouch finishes its journey down the line. It's a muted celebration because everyone is exhausted. Inessa Spring's team shuts down their computers, breaks down the folding tables, disconnects cables, and gathers their belongings to head out the door. They congratulate one another on getting through another grueling election. They have shown me what democracy really looks like.

10:00 P.M. Cassie Klosterman is waiting outside the tab room for final results, so she can post them on social media. Everything regarding tabulation has gone perfectly until now. Checking their totals, the tabulation team has discovered that one polling-place team has not turned in their flash drive. They left it in the scanner, something that trainers had warned against over and over in class. In a session I attended, trainer Kevin

McCloskey told the class to remove the flash drive before they did anything else. "Then take it straight to the orange pouch," he said. "Do not pass Go. Do not collect $200. Do not put it in your pocket or set it down on a table."

Without that single flash drive, the results are incomplete. A staffer offers to go back to the polling site, open up the transport cage, unlock the scanner, and retrieve the flash drive. But the polling place is already locked, and nobody's home.

"Paper ballots to the rescue!" says Julie Leicht. The last problem of a day plagued by glitches is the one that ultimately proves one of the main selling points of the ballot-on-demand system. They have full, accessible backup. All they need to do to complete the day's count is to scan the paper ballots from the missing polling place. And that's easy because the duffel holding them is ensconced in the precisely labeled storage system in the warehouse. Fifteen minutes later, the tally is complete.

10:15 P.M. Final results posted. In election-management circles, the election director's prayer is "Dear Lord, don't let it be close." Tonight, for Fey and Stream, that entreaty has been answered. The lopsided results of the presidential primaries mean that there's little chance of a challenge, and no need for a do-over. Sighs of relief and congratulations all around.

Everybody except the top administrators and the tab-room team have gone home. An outsider wandering into the tomblike silence of the deserted office might not even realize that, just minutes ago, it had been ground zero for a hectic, challenging, uniquely troublesome—but ultimately successful—election day.

This election day is in the books, but there is still work to be done. By law, jurisdictions have two weeks to certify the election and report official results. With a brief reprieve—a late start time of 10 a.m.—the office will be back to work tomorrow to start the post-election verifications and accounting that button it all up. The warehouse (now logistics) crew will spend the next six days hauling the transport cages back to the warehouse, unloading the contents, untangling miles of extension cords, and, in the virus-infected world of March 2020, wiping it all down with antibacterial solution. They will need to move fast. They and everyone else in the office need to reboot the whole pre-election regimen immediately. The countywide municipal elections will take place in just three weeks.

■

Or, maybe not.

MARCH 14, 2020. Everything may be about to change, and some of the carefully wrought procedures that have made elections tick in St. Louis County may be about to morph or perhaps become obsolete. In a surprise, coronavirus-driven plot twist, four days after the election, the St. Louis County Board of Commissioners files a petition with the Missouri Circuit Court of Appeals, asking to postpone the April 7 municipal elections until April 28, and to allow it to be a mail-in election. Like many jurisdictions caught in the pandemic pandemonium of 2020, St. Louis County election leaders are worrying about the health risk to voters and workers of gathering at polling places or waiting in lines.

But Missouri statutes don't provide for the kind of vote-by-mail structure that has been adopted in Colorado, Hawaii, Oregon, Washington, and Utah, and on the wish list of other states as well. A quirk in Missouri election law makes it possible to hold a mail-in election, but only under very narrow, special circumstances. Missouri election statutes allow a mail-in election only if it is a vote on a local issue, it is non-partisan, and has no candidates on the ballot. Those provisions won't help St. Louis County justify the mail-in election they are seeking. But they did enable the town of Tightwad, Missouri (population sixty-seven, as of 2017), to have a mail-in election on a local tax issue in 2019.

MARCH 16, 2020. The court turns down the election board's petition for an April 28 mail-in election.

MARCH 18, 2020. Governor Mike Parson signs an executive order calling for all Missouri municipal elections to be postponed until June 2. The order doesn't authorize the hoped-for mail-in election. But it helpfully extends the deadline to apply for an absentee ballot, allows for in-person absentee voting until the day before the election, and makes 7 p.m. on election day the deadline for absentee ballots to arrive in election offices. Voting-rights advocates are lobbying for no-excuse absentee voting, but the governor and secretary of state are not willing to go that far. Each of these accommodations will have implications for staffing and logistics.

MARCH 23, 2020. In further response to the COVID-19 pandemic, St. Louis County government leaders issue a stay-at-home order, throwing day-to-day election operations and future planning into even more uncertainty. Considered an essential service, the election office must remain open. To maintain social distancing, Stream and Fey split the office staff into two groups and implement a one-week-on, one-week-off schedule. Workers sanitize doorknobs, handles, countertops, and other exposed surfaces multiple times per day. During their weekly shifts, "doctors" Rick Stream and Eric Fey take charge of checking workers' temperatures at the beginning and end of each day, a responsibility they could never have contemplated.

APRIL 10, 2020. Three days after the municipal election day that wasn't, the election office is engaged in yet another unprecedented activity. To protect voters and workers, the election board will be encouraging absentee voting. Today, they are mass mailing absentee-ballot applications to every registered voter over the age of sixty in St. Louis County. There are 230,000 of them. Each envelope contains three color-coded applications— one for each of the next three elections in 2020.

Under Missouri rules, voters will still have to indicate their reason for voting absentee. Fortunately, they won't have to lie. One of the already acceptable reasons is illness or the need to take care of another sick person. The wording doesn't include being locked down by government fiat or voluntarily engaging in social distancing. But it's probably close enough, and as Rick Stream says in a media interview, "We don't have election police who monitor whether you're actually ill that day."

Having never before done a mass mailing of this scope, Fey can't predict how many applications they will receive. "I can only make what my grandfather would call 'SWAG,' meaning 'some wild-ass guess," says Fey. "But I wouldn't be surprised if we get 50,000 or more, compared to the 14,000 we processed for the presidential primary last month. The effect on our operations will be significant."

Other jurisdictions across the country are contemplating changes as well, and voting-rights activists have begun calling for a permanent, nationwide switch to mail-in elections. My own up-close observations of the labor-intensive, manual work that goes into processing absentee ballots make me think that all-mail voting is easier said than done. States that already conduct mail-in elections have staffing configurations and elaborate security and processing regimens that many jurisdictions have not yet imagined and may find difficult to put into place.

In a normal world, three days after an election, Fey would be tying up loose ends and gearing up organizationally, logistically and psychologically for the next go-round. This year, he is no longer sure what normal is. He has told me many times that the one constant in election administration is change. But perhaps not this much or at this pace. "I can't even predict what's going to happen next week," he said. "It's changing minute by minute."

Epilogue

THE ELECTION CYCLE IS an infinite loop, so there is no end to this story. Many things changed between my first inquiries to St. Louis County election leadership and my most recent observations. Some of the people featured here have retired, have been promoted within the department, or have moved on. Their stories still count as examples of what it takes, both institutionally and individually, to pull elections together.

At this writing, the coronavirus pandemic is causing uncertainty everywhere, including in election world. Administrators in every jurisdiction across the country are scrambling to adapt. But having talked with, observed, and learned from some of the best, I feel confident that, whatever shape elections take in the future, the people I have come to know in St. Louis County, and others like them all over the United States, will be there for us and for our democracy.

In early 2019, when I started this endeavor, I met with some resistance that made me momentarily doubt the value of what I was hoping to do. During my presidential primary election-day observation, a board member confided that, when I first proposed the idea for this book, she and the other commissioners didn't take me seriously. "We thought, 'Sure, let her come to some meetings and interview a few people. She'll probably be gone in a month or two,'" she said. "We didn't know how committed you would turn out to be." She made my day.

Early on, I had also called a prominent voting-rights activist for input. I'm not naming names, and it's not someone quoted or even mentioned in this book. When I described my idea, the response was, "It sounds like a colossal waste of time." Taken aback at first, I decided to turn those words into a challenge. If you've gotten all the way to this epilogue, and if anything you've read has made you think "I had no idea," or has prompted you to ask yourself, "I wonder how they do that where I vote," I will consider this effort a success that has proven the naysayers wrong. Thank you for sharing in my journey.

I have learned that election jurisdictions come in a variety of shapes and sizes, and that elections have infinite, unpredictable variations from cycle to cycle. The one constant is the person who comes to a polling place or a vote center, pushes the buttons on a ballot-marking device or a touchscreen, fills in the ovals on a paper ballot, or votes absentee. It's you, the voter. The election insiders you've met in this book are working hard to make your vote count. They are our partners in democracy. But you have the ultimate power. Please use it.

Acknowledgments

I COULD NOT HAVE EVEN BEGUN THIS BOOK without the encouragement of my husband, Arthur Lieber. He was enthusiastic from the get-go, nurtured me through my self-doubts, listened as I bounced ideas around, and was my earliest reader and booster. All of this while he was writing his own book: acts of love that mean the world to me.

I can't say enough good things about Eric Fey, whose experiences and observations figure prominently in this book. When I first encountered him a few years ago, it was instantly clear that he was one of the good guys and a forward-thinking election administrator. The idea for this book sprang from a tour he led at election headquarters. He was the first person I approached with the concept, and he supported it immediately. He was my go-to person throughout my research and shepherded me through the ins and outs.

This project would not have been possible without the cooperation of the entire leadership team of the St. Louis Board of Elections: Eric Fey, Rick Stream, Julie Leicht, and Christian Tolbert. They smoothed the way, educated me, and made my work enjoyable. I learned something new every time I visited the office. Thanks also to the commissioners on the Board of Elections: Sharon Buchanan-McClure, Matthew Potter, Trudi

McCollum Foushee, and Peggy Barnhart. I learned a great deal from each of them. Thank you for your trust.

I am deeply grateful to all the St. Louis County election workers who agreed to talk with me and share their stories. I was continuously impressed by their professionalism, their diligence, and their ability to roll with the many punches that punctuate life in the world of elections. To my surprise, it turned out that I could never tell who was a D and who was an R, unless they told me. That phenomenon is a reassuring testament to their dedication to the work, rather than to party identity and politics. Thank you Amy Blankenship, Daryl Brown, Kay Buchanan, Maureen Callahan, Cindy Carberry, Beau Coker, Amber Cole, Haley Colter, Melanie Craig, Theresa Dintleman, Marie Ellison, Lori Fiegel, Cliff Freebersyser, Zach Goldford, Matt Harms, Bill Hartnett, Stephanie Hegger, Craig Hite, Ryan Hunt, LaTasha Jackson, Cassie Klosterman, Peggy Kochner, Linda Kuchar, Linda McLain, Kevin McCloskey, Matt McLaughlin, Al Molitor, John Moore, Melissa Moore, Rosemarie Moss, Tim Peterson, Rob Ryan, Ray Schindler, Inessa Spring, Hannah Talley, Ron Wagoner, Leigh Ann Warrington, and Joe Winter.

To election staffers in St. Louis County with whom I didn't have formal interviews or casual conversations, and to the thousands of other election workers around the country who work in the background, you deserve recognition as well. Your work, mostly unseen by the public, is essential to maintaining the fairness and integrity of elections. You are not invisible. I see you, and I hope this book will help readers appreciate your work, too.

Several people took the time to walk with me through my initial concept and outline, and to read my manuscript as it developed. First among them is my sister, Renee Shur, my confidante and an idea person extraordinaire. We logged many hours of phone consultations—not always on topic—and I could always count on her for encouragement and honest, constructive criticism. Also, her knowledge of the rules of style kept my punctuation, capitalization, and italicization honest. She held my hand—long distance—and pushed me forward when I needed it most.

Thanks to early reader Bill Kesler, my political-campaign comrade, a talented photojournalist, and someone who has played a key role in keeping our political blog, Occasional Planet.com, alive and on track for ten years. His suggestions for improvements to my manuscript made a difference. I value his friendship and his savvy. His enthusiasm for my work has buoyed me.

Michael W. Robbins graciously agreed to a close early reading of my manuscript. His effort exceeded my expectations. He used his considerable skills as a longtime magazine editor to analyze its pluses and minuses and to make my writing better. Encouragement from someone with his credentials is affirming and inspiring.

I received very helpful feedback from John Messmer, who reviewed my manuscript from the perspective of a political science professor, a political reformer, and a former candidate for US Congress.

When I asked Hilene Bilchik if she wanted to read my manuscript piece by piece, she eagerly dived in. Her positive feedback was a game-changer.

Eva Bochem-Shur, my niece, jumped at the chance to design the cover of this book. I was correct in thinking that working with her—such a politically tuned-in, intelligent, talented, and creative graphic designer—would be productive and fun. Peggy Nehmen, of Nehmen-Kodner Design, made the inside pages readable and inviting, and she was generous in sharing her inside knowledge of the publishing world, steering me away from the pitfalls and guiding me toward smarter strategies. Kelly Santaguida and Tony Chellini at Gatekeeper Press created a uniquely flexible publishing framework for my project and were very understanding and fair when the rules of engagement changed.

Although I have never met her, best-selling writer Susan Orlean provided inspiration for this project. After reading *The Library Book*, a remarkably accessible inside look at the Los Angeles Public Library, I began thinking about a similar approach to election administration. I can only hope that my story is half as engaging as hers.

Finally, thanks to my family, the Bilchiks—Kevin, Kendall, Eileen, Mia, Eli, and Hilene—whose love and encouragement mean everything to me. I know Warren would have been proud of me, too, but he didn't make it to the finish line. I have dedicated this book to his memory.

Bibliography

YOU WILL UNDOUBTEDLY NOTICE that this is a very lengthy bibliography. I consulted many sources in researching this book, but not all of them are directly referenced in the text. However, in an era in which "fake news" has become a charge often unfairly leveled against legitimate journalism, it has become more important than ever to reassure the reader that quotations are accurate and that assertions of fact can be checked.

Ackerman, S.J. "The Vote That Failed," *Smithsonian Magazine*, November 1998.

Andersen, L.V. "Insanely High Turnout Reveals Voting Problems Across the Country — Here's What's Going On," *Digg*, November 6, 2018.

Associated Press. "Louisiana's Ballot Will Feature Unusual Candidate Nicknames," *U.S. News*, August 9, 2019.

Ayala, Rebecca, "Voting Problems 2018," Brennan Center for Justice, November 5, 2018.

Ayala, Rebecca and Myrna Perez. "Here We Go Again: Politicians Using the False Specter of Voter Fraud," Brennan Center for Justice, November 19, 2019.

Bach, Natasha. "Millions of Americans Have Been Purged from Voter Rolls—and May Not Even Realize It," *Fortune*, January 14, 2010.

Bailey, Heather. "New Voting System Rolled Out for 2020," SonomaWest. com, January 29, 2020.

Bajak, Frank. "Reliability of Pricey New Voting Machines Questioned," *St. Louis Post-Dispatch*, February 23, 2020.

Ballotpedia. "Signature Requirements for Ballot Measures in Missouri," 2019.

Barrington, Russell. "Signatures Are Obsolete: Replacing the Illegible Squiggly Line," Medium, March 14, 2018.

BBC. "US Election: 10 US Election Oddities," November 3, 2016.

BBC. "Indonesia Election: More than 270 Election Staff Die Counting Votes," BBC.com, April 28, 2019.

Belarmino, Mike, and Austin Ingeheart. "Fact Sheet on Counties' Role in the Election Process," National Association of Counties, November 8, 2016.

Berkowitz, Bonnie. "Think You'll Know Who Won on Election Night? Not So Fast …," *Washington Post*, October 29, 2018.

Bernstein, Sharon, and Grant Smith. "Ahead of November Election, Old Voting Machines Stir Concerns among U.S. Officials," *Reuters*, May 21, 2018.

Bernthal, Jeff. "St. Louis County Election Board Director Apologizes for Election Day Mistakes," Fox2 News, April 6, 2016.

Blaze, Matt, Harri Hursti, et al. "DEF CON 27, Voting Machine Hacking Village," Defcon.org, August 2019.

Boughton, Melissa. "NC Board of Elections Recommends Salary Increase for Executive Director," NC Policy Watch, May 23, 2019.

Brody, Lisa. "New Clerk Resigns before Taking City Position," *Downtown Newsmagazine*, Birmingham/Bloomfield, January 3, 2020.

Brooks, David. "Lawmakers Dig through Legal Consequences of Snowy Town Voting Mess," *Concord Monitor*, March 21, 2017.

Bump, Philip. "Let's See What Happens If We Take the Unserious Background-Checks-for-Voter-Registration Idea Seriously," *Washington Post*, September 12, 2017.

Bunch, Riley. "Special Elections Small Test for Voting System Ahead of Presidential Primary," *Valdosta Daily Times*, January 24, 2020.

Cagle, Susie. "How Voter Fraud Works – And Mostly Doesn't," *ProPublica*, November 3, 2016.

Campbell, Tracy. *Deliver the Vote: A History of Election Fraud, an American Tradition 1724 – 2004*, New York: Carroll & Graff Publishers, 2005.

CareerCast. "The Most Stressful Jobs of 2018."

Carney, Jordain. "Senate Passes Bill Making Hacking Voting Systems a Federal Crime," *The Hill*, July 17, 2019.

Chapin, Doug. "Crash into Me: Electionline Weekly on Phenomenon of Cars into Polling Places," University of Minnesota Election Academy, August 16, 2019.

Chapin, Doug. "This is the End: Lackawanna Recycles Touchscreen Voting Machines," University of Minnesota Election Academy, June 27, 2016.

Chen, M. Keith, Kareem Haggag, et al. "Racial Disparities in Voting Wait Times: Evidence from Smartphone Data," Cornell University, August 30, 2019.

Chisnell, Dana and Whitney Queensbery. "Security Insights and Issues for Poll Workers," Center for Civic Design, October 18, 2014.

Chokshi, Nira. "Hackers Are Holding Baltimore Hostage: How They Struck and What's Next," *New York Times*, May 22, 2019.

Clark, Christine. "Can Americans Trust Elections?" UC San Diego, November 2, 2018.

Cohen, Ilana. "The Power of Ballot Initiatives," *Harvard Political Review*, December 10, 2018.

Cooperman, Jeannette. "St. Louis' Great Divorce: A Complete History of the City and County Separation and Attempts to Get Back Together," *St. Louis Magazine*, March 8, 2019.

Currier, Joel. "Three Charged with Election Fraud in St. Louis County," *St. Louis Post-Dispatch*, August 28, 2013.

Dalesio, Emery P. "Who's behind Voting Machine Makers? Money of Unclear Origins," *AP News*, July 12, 2019.

Danetz, Lisa. "Improving Motor Voter Registration," Electionline, July 25, 2019.

DeBats, Don. "Public Voting before the Secret Ballot," Social Logic, University of Virginia, 2020.

Deere, Stephen, and Doug Moore. "Prosecutors, FBI Investigating Allegations of Absentee Vote Fraud in Berkeley," *St. Louis Post-Dispatch*, October 24, 2016.

Denkmann, Libby. "Beverly Hills Sues over 'Severe Ballot Design Flaw' in LA County Voting Machines," LAist, January 23, 2020.

Denkmann, Libby. "State Oks LA County's New Voting Machines—With A Whole Lot of Caveats," LAist, January 25, 2020.

Desilver, Drew. "Weekday Elections Set the U.S. Apart from Many Other Advanced Democracies," Pew Research Center, FacTank, November 6, 2018.

Devine, Curt and Drew Griffin. "Election Error May Have Cost Georgia Representative His Race," CNN, September 10, 2018.

Disability Rights Section, US Department of Justice. "Solutions for Five Common ADA Access Problems at Polling Places," ada.gov.

Doiron, Alexa. "The Work Doesn't Stop at the Registrar's Office after Elections Are Done. It Keeps Going, Fully Staffed or Not," *Williamsburg Yorktown Daily*, January 25, 2020.

Donnell, Ryan. "You Voted Where? Unusual Polling Places in America," Governing, October 2016.

Doty, Grant. "Three Voting Myths that Should Not Keep You Home on Election Day," *St. Louis American*, November 1, 2018.

Douglas, Joshua A. "A 'Checklist Manifesto' for Election Day: How to Prevent Mistakes at the Polls," University of Kentucky, UKnowledge, Winter 2016.

Downey, KC. "Town-by-Town New Hampshire Snow Totals: March 14-15, 2017," WMUR9, March 15, 2017.

Dynamic St. Louis. "Mound City on the Mississippi—A St. Louis History," St. Louis Historic Preservation Agency.

Election Assistance Commission. "Election Management Guidelines," EAC. gov.

Ehresman, Brodie. "R2 Certified Electronic Voting Machine Recycling, Advanced Technology Recycling," 2018.

Epps, Garrett. "What Does the Constitution Actually Say About Voting Rights?" *Atlantic*, August 19, 2013.

Fair Vote. "Right to Vote Amendment," FairVote.org, accessed January 31, 2020.

Fenster, Jordan. "The Three Craziest Things to Happen on Election Day in Connecticut," *CT Post,* November 6, 2019.

Fessler, Pam. "Election Officials to Convene Amid Historic Focus on Voting and Interference," NPR, January 27, 2020.

Fessler, Pam. "States Upgrade Election Equipment — Wary of 'A Race without a Finish Line,'" NPR, September 3, 2019.

Fessler, Pam. "Trips to Vegas and Chocolate-Covered Pretzels: Election Vendors Come under Scrutiny," NPR, May 2, 2019.

Fischer, Howard. "Rep. Finchem Bill Proposes Electronic Signatures for Ballot Measures," *Arizona Capitol Times*, December 31, 2018.

Fleischer, Jodie, Katie Leslie, and Jeff Piper. "Prince George's Ballot Shortages More Widespread Than Previously Thought," NBC Washington, November 19, 2018.

Fortier, John C., et al. "Reducing Polling Place Wait Times by Measuring Lines and Managing Polling Place Resources," Bipartisan Policy Center, April 2018.

Fowler, Stephen. "Some Voting Machine Issues Present in Southwest Georgia Special Election," GPBnews.org, January 29, 2020.

Fuller, Jaime. "If You Give a Mouse a Vote," *American Prospect*, November 5, 2013.

Giegerich, Steve. "St. Louis County Elections Debacle Spawns a Suspension and an Offer to Resign," *St. Louis Post-Dispatch*, April 19, 2016.

Giegerich, Steve. "St. Louis County Suffers Voting Problems, Voting Confusion," *St. Louis Post-Dispatch*, April 6, 2016.

Glum, Julia. "You Can Make Some Quick Cash on Election Day by Being a Poll Worker. Here's How Much It Pays," *Money*, October 29, 2018.

Goggin, Benjamin. "Long Lines, Broken Machines, and Gun Scares — Here Are the Reported Problems Voters Are Experiencing during the Midterms," Business Insider, November 6, 2018.

Goldstein, Dana, and Kirk Johnson. "Voters Weigh In on Key Issues through More than 150 Ballot Initiatives," *New York Times*, November 6, 2018.

Green, Mary. "Linn County Using Heat Maps to Increase Efficiency for 2020 Elections," KCRG.com, January 29, 2020.

Groeger, Lena V. "Disenfranchised by Bad Design," *ProPublica,* October 20, 2016.

Gross, Terry. "Election Meltdown Is a Real Possibility in 2020 Presidential Race, Author Warns," NPR, January 29, 2020.

Hall, Thad E, Quin Monson, and Kelly D. Patterson. "The Human Dimensions of Elections: How Poll Workers Shape Public Confidence in Elections," *Political Research Quarterly,* vol. 62, no.3, September 2009.

Herron, Michael C., Michael D. Martinez, and Daniel A. Smith. "Ballot Design, Voter Intentions, and Representation: A Study of the 2018 Midterm Election in Florida," UPenn.edu, July 1, 2019.

Holder, Sarah. "In New York, Citywide Technical Difficulties Deter Some from Voting," *Citylab,* November 6, 2018.

Horn, Dan. "100 Poll Workers Fired for Not Voting," *Cincinnati Enquirer,* February 11, 2015.

Horseman, Jeff. "California Wants New Voting Machines for Next Year: Riverside County Will Have to Spend to Do It," *Press-Enterprise,* March 4, 2019.

Houston, Matt. "How Candidates Use Nicknames to Earn Your Vote," WAFB.com, September 13, 2019.

Howard, Elizabeth, and Christopher Deluzio. "Defending Elections: Federal Funding Needs for State Election Security," Brennan Center for Justice, July 18, 2019.

Humphrey School of Public Affairs. "Certificate in Election Administration," University of Minnesota, 2020.

Hurley, Erin. "All Elections Are Local: The County Role in the Elections Process," National Association of Counties, November 6, 2018.

Huskerson, Tom. "A Brief History of Voter Registration in the United States," *Independent Voter News,* September 8, 2014.

Hutt, Rosamond. "These Are the Countries with the Highest Voter Turnout," World Economic Forum, November 7, 2018.

Hyde, Charles A. "Why Museums Should Be Proud Polling Sites," *Smithsonian*, October 29, 2018.

Immel, Crystin. "Ten of the Most Interesting Polling Places in Chicago," WTTW.com, November 5, 2018.

Ingraham, Christopher. "A Terrifying and Hilarious Map of Squirrel Attacks on the U.S. Power Grid," *Washington Post*, January 12, 2016.

Ingraham, Christopher. "Thousands of Polling Places Were Closed over the Past Decade. Here's Where," *Washington Post*, October 26, 2018.

Issa, Nader. "New Illinois Law Excuses Students from Class So They Can Go Vote," *Chicago Sun-Times*, January 23, 2020.

Itkowitz, Colby. "Democrats Sue Three Battleground States over Law That GOP Candidates' Names Be Listed First on Ballot," *Washington Post*, November 1, 2019.

Jones, Douglas W. "Chad—From Waste Product to Headline," University of Iowa Department of Computer Science, uiowa.edu, 2002.

Kamiya, Gary. "1856 Vigilantes Changed Corrupt Political System," *SF Gate*, August 1, 2014.

Kanengiser, Henry. "In New York, Where You Live Can Determine How Hard It Is to Vote," *City Limits*, April 25, 2019.

Kauffman, Johnny. "Six Takeaways from Georgia's 'Use It Or Lose It' Voter Purge Investigation," NPR, October 22, 2018.

Kazanjian, Glynis, and Len Lazarick. "Scanner Shortage Caused Lines and Long Waits Election Day," MarylandReporter.com, November 14, 2016.

Kelly, Jon. "Is a Signature Still Useful?" *BBC News Magazine*, May 7, 2014.

Keyssar, Alexander. *The Right to Vote: The Contested History of Democracy in America*, New York: Basic Books, 2000.

Khalid, Asma, Don Gonyea, and Leila Fadel. "On the Sidelines of Democracy: Exploring Why So Many People Don't Vote," NPR, September 10, 2018.

Kilpatrick, Mary. "After the Polls Close on Election Day, Here's How the Cuyahoga County Board of Elections Counts Your Vote," Cleveland.com, September 10, 2019.

Kimball, David C., and Brady Baybeck. "Are All Jurisdictions Equal? Size Disparity in Election Administration," *Election Law Journal*, vol. 12, no. 2, 2013.

Kimball, David C., and Martha Kropf. "The Street-Level Bureaucrats of Elections: Selection Methods for Local Election Officials, *Review of Policy Research*, vol. 23, no. 6, 2006.

Kimel, Earle. "Precinct in Sarasota County Opens without Proper Ballots," *Herald-Tribune*, November 6, 2018.

King, Elizabeth. "How the U.S. Ended Up with Today's Paper Ballots," *Time*, April 26, 2016.

Kirby, Jen. "Why It Takes So Long to Get Election Night Results," Vox, November 6, 2018.

Kliegman, Julie. "Eleven Unusual U.S. Polling Places," Mental Floss, February 19, 2016.

Kohler, Jeremy. "Creve Coeur Mayor Barry Glantz Fails to Gather Enough Signatures to Enter County Council Race," *St. Louis Post-Dispatch*, July 5, 2019.

Kousser, Thad, Eric McGhee, and Mindy Romero. "Op-Ed: Say Goodbye to Your Local Precinct. Voting in California Is About to Change Dramatically," *Los Angeles Times*, May 31, 2019.

Laird, Susan. "California Museum Tells the Story of Golden State Voting," *Village Life Newspaper*, August 8, 2016.

Laitner, Bill. "Ballot Shortages Reported in Oakland County; Voters Told to Wait," *Detroit Free Press*, August 7, 2018.

Lapowsky, Issie. "States Need Way More Money to Fix Crumbling Voting Machines," *Wired*, March 5, 2019.

Latimer, Craig. "Requirements: Make an Impact. Be a Poll Worker," Hillsborough County Website, 2019.

Leavenworth, Jesse, and Dave Altimari. "Official: Hartford Mixup a Failure of Elections 101," *Hartford Courant*, November 4, 2014.

Leip, Dave. "Atlas of U.S. Presidential Elections," uselectionatlas.org, 2004–2018.

Leovy, Jill. "The Computer Scientist Who Prefers Paper," *Atlantic*, December 2017.

Lepore, Jill. "Rock, Paper, Scissors: How We Used to Vote," *New Yorker*, October 6, 2008.

Levy, Pema. "It's Not Just Kobach: Three Vote-Suppressing Secretaries of State Are Overseeing Their Own Elections," *Mother Jones*, August 11, 2018.

Lindeman, Mark, and Philip B. Stark. "A Gentle Introduction to Risk Limiting Audits," *IEEE Security and Privacy*, Special Issue on Electronic Voting, March 2012.

Lopez, Ashley. "Old Voting Machines Confuse Some Texans during Midterm Election," NPR, October 30, 2018.

Lynch, Dylan. "What's in a Name When It's on a Ballot?" National Conference of State Legislatures, May 3, 2018.

Lyons, Kathryn. "Ugly Gerry Wants You to Know the 'Ugly' Truth about Gerrymandering," *Roll Call*, August 2, 2019.

MacDougall, Ian. "What Went Wrong at New York City Polling Places? It Was Something in the Air. Literally," *ProPublica*, November 6, 2018.

Madej, Patricia. "Why Philly Has More than 800 Polling Places and Why Some Are Just, Well, Strange," *Inquirer*, November 3, 2018.

Maggi, Laura. "Protecting US Elections Needs Much More Federal Money: Report," Defense One, July 22, 2019.

Mahoney, John. "State Partisan Composition," National Council of State Legislatures, November 22, 2019.

Maldonado, Laura. "Three Kings County Precincts Receive Ballots in Error," *Hanford Sentinel*, February 24, 2020.

Mandell, Lisa Johnson. "Wife Steps In to Help United Van Lines CEO on 'Undercover Boss,'" AOL, March 11, 2015.

Massachusetts Institute of Technology. "Elections Performance Index," Election Lab.

McLean, Danielle. "Democrats Sue over a Florida Law that Puts Trump's Name ahead of Rivals on the 2020 Ballot," *ThinkProgress*, July 16, 2019.

McCormack, Kathy. "Dixville Notch Finds Enough People to Keep First-in-the-Nation Voting Title," NECN.com, January 9, 2020.

Mehrotra, Kartikay. "State, Local Officials Face Challenge in Updating Old, Insecure Voting Machines," Bloomberg, January 3, 2020.

Menarndt, Aubrey. "I'm an Elections Monitor. The United States Isn't Like Other Countries," *New York Times*, May 8, 2019.

Menengus, Bryan. "Voting Machine Hell, 2018: A Running List of Election Glitches, Malfunctions, and Screwups," Gizmodo, November 6, 2018.

MIT, Election Data Science Lab. "Voter Confidence," 2019.

Monahan, Kevin, Ben Popken, et al. "LA County Builds Its New Voting Machines from Scratch. Will They Be Ready?" NBC News, February 14, 2020.

Morley, Michael T. "Election Emergencies: Voting in the Wake of Natural Disasters and Terrorist Attacks," *Emory Law Journal*, vol. 67, Iss. 3, 2018.

Munks, Jamie, and Rick Pearson. "Candidates After Top Ballot Position Line Up Early as Illinois' 2020 Election Season Gets Underway," *Chicago Tribune*, November 25, 2019.

Murillo, Mike. "'It Won't Ever Happen Again': What Officials Learned from Prince George's Co. Ballot Shortage," WTOP, November 7, 2018.

Nagourney, Adam. "After the Attacks: Election; Primary Rescheduled for Sept. 25, with Runoff, if Necessary, Set for Oct. 11," *New York Times*, September 14, 2001.

Nardelli, Alberto, Denis Dizidic, and Elvira Jukic. "Bosnia and Herzegovina - The World's Most Complicated System of Government?" *Guardian,* October 8, 2014.

National Association of Secretaries of State. "GIS and the Future of Voter Registration Systems," NASS.org, Winter 2019.

National Conference of State Legislatures. "Election Administration at State and Local Levels," June 15, 2016.

National Conference of State Legislatures. "Election Costs: What States Pay," August 3, 2018.

National Conference of State Legislatures. "Election Emergencies," November 12, 2018.

National Conference of State Legislatures. "Voter Information: Varied State Requirements," NCSL.org/research.

National Conference of State Legislatures. "Voting System Paper Trail Requirements," NCSL.org, June 27, 2019.

National Conference of State Legislators. "The Election Administrator's Perspective," NCSL.org, February 24, 2017.

National Conference of State Legislators. "The Facts on Ten Common Election Misconceptions," *The Canvass*, Is. 63, October 2015.

National Conference of State Legislatures. "2015 Election Legislation Enacted by State Legislatures," January 27, 2016.

Naylor, Brian. "Sign Here: Why Elections Officials Struggle to Match Voters' Signatures," NPR, November 17, 2018.

Newman, Lily Hay. "Hackers Take on Darpa's $10 Million Voting Machine," *Wired*, September 9, 2019.

Nichols, John. "Time for a 'Right to Vote' Constitutional Amendment," *Nation*, March 5, 2013.

Niesse, Mark. "Few Voters Check Printed Ballots Like Those in Georgia, Study Shows," *Atlanta Journal Constitution*, January 9, 2020.

Nilsen, Ella. "It's Not the First Time a Blizzard and Town Meeting Day Have Coincided," *Concord Monitor*, March 14, 2017.

Norden, Lawrence. "America's Voting Technology Crisis," Brennan Center for Justice, September 15, 2015.

Novick, Andy. "The EAC Lied, Lever Voting Machines (Almost) Died," Brad-Blog, March 2, 2009.

O'Donoghue, Julie. "St. Louis County Voters to Mostly Use Paper Ballots," St. Louis Public Radio, September 3, 2019.

Ola, Mary Jo. "Poll Workers to Get Trained for an Active Attacker Situation," TMJ4.com, January 9, 2020.

O'Neill, Tim. "Aug. 22, 1876: How the 'Great Divorce' of St. Louis City and St. Louis County Started," *St. Louis Post-Dispatch*, August 22, 2019.

Ouriel, Andy. "Sandusky's Gov't Eliminates Columbus Day as Holiday," *Sandusky Register*, January 30, 2019.

Padilla, Alex. "Randomized Alphabet," California Secretary of State Website, 2020.

Parks, Miles. "Why Elections Officials Aren't Taking a Simple Security Step," NPR, January 26, 2020.

Patrick, Tammy. "Increasing Trust in Elections: Democracy Fund's Election Validation Project," Democracy Fund, May 29, 2018.

Patrick, Tammy. "Knowing It's Right," Electionline, May 23, 2019.

Patrick, Tammy. "Leave No Voter Behind: Implications of the US' Withdrawal from the Universal Postal Union," Electionline, August 1, 2019.

Pete, Joseph S. "Poll Workers Help 86-Year-Old Voter Find His Lost Wedding Ring," *Northwest Indiana Times*, November 6, 2019.

Pettigrew, Stephen. "The Racial Gap in Wait Times: Why Minority Precincts Are Underserved by Local Election Officials," *Political Science Quarterly*, vol. 132, no.3, 2017.

Pew Center on the States. "Poll Worker Pay," 2012.

Pfeiffer, Stuart. "L.A. County May Stick with Inka Vote Ballots," *Los Angeles Times*, November 5, 2004.

Pratt, Timothy, and Undark. "Computer Scientists Make the Case against an Expensive New Voting System," *Atlantic*, July 13, 2019

Pryor, Ben. "How Different Polling Locations Subconsciously Influence Voters", *Scientific American*, February 29, 2016.

Ramachandran, Gowri, and Susannah Goodman. "The Simple Lessons from a Complicated Iowa Caucus," Just Security, February 14, 2020.

Reuters. "What's in a Name? One-Third of US Voters Don't Know Candidates," CNBC, October 3, 2018.

Riley, Michael, and Jordan Robertson. "Russian Hacks on U.S. Voting System Wider Than Previously Known," Bloomberg, June 13, 2017.

Robertson, Gary D. "Absentee Vote Changes May Have Invited 'Ballot Harvesting,'" *APNews*, December 7, 2018.

Rodriguez, Rosa Salter. "Black Boxes Increase Voting Device Security,*"Journal Gazette*, January 27, 2020.

Rohrbach, Hope. "Ballot Measures | Go or No-Go Decisions," The Campaign Workshop, April 25, 2019.

Rosenbaum, Jason. "On the Trail: What Went Wrong during St. Louis County's Municipal Elections?" St. Louis Public Radio, April 6, 2016.

Rosenfeld, Steven. "America Refuses to Fix Its Broken Election System," Independent Media Institute, June 6, 2019.

Rosenfeld, Steven. "Voting Booth Special Report: The Future of Vote Count-Verifying Technologies," Independent Media Institute, December 17, 2018.

Rosenfeld, Steven. "Why a Local Showdown Over Voting Technology in N.C. Is a Harbinger for Elections across the U.S.," Salon, September 29, 2018.

Rosenfeld, Steven. "Why over 130,000 New Voting Machines Could Lead to More Distrust in U.S. Elections," Salon, October 8, 2019.

Rosenstone, Steven J., and Raymond E. Wolfinger. "The Effect of Voter Registration Laws on Voter Turnout," pp. 22–45, University of California, Berkeley, 1978.

Rothschild, Mike. "Wacky Election Facts from Around the World," Ranker, 2020.

Rubin, Jennifer. "Is It a Problem When Voters Think an Election Will Be Rigged?" *Washington Post*, August 2, 2018.

Russell, Barrington. "Signatures Are Obsolete: Replacing the Illegible Squiggly Line," Medium, March 14, 2018.

Samilton, Tracy. "Bill Introduced to Ease Expected Problems with Counting Absentee Ballots," Michigan Radio, January 28, 2020.

Sanchez, Gabriel. "Here Are Some of the Wild Places That People Voted at Today," BuzzFeed News, November 6, 2018.

Scarr, Simon, Manas Sharma, and Marco Hernandez. "Roads, Boats, Elephants: How India Mobilised a Million Polling Stations," Reuters, May 22, 2019.

Scott, Eugene. "Sanders: Arizonans Waiting Five Hours to Vote is 'a Disgrace,'" CNN, March 23, 2016.

Shafer, Jack. "Stolen Election—As American as Apple Pie," *Slate Magazine*, October 21, 2008.

Shapiro, Eliza. "RIP, Lever Voting Machines," *Daily Beast*, July 14, 2017.

Shellman, Dwight, and Jennifer Morrell. "Colorado's Implementation of Risk-Limiting Audits," U.S. Election Assistance Commission, October 30, 2017.

Shorman, Jonathan, and Steve Vockrodt. "Dodge City's Out-of-Town Polling Place Adds to Fears of Voter Suppression in Kansas," *Wichita Eagle*, October 26, 2018.

Slack, Donovan, Bart Jansen, et al. "Problems at Polls? Irregularities, Malfunctions in Georgia, Texas, Indiana, Other States," *USA Today*, November 6, 2018.

Smith, Adam. "India Elections: Snake Stuck in a Polling Machine Sparks Panic and Holds Up Voting," *Express*, April 23, 2019.

Smith, Sherman. "Congressional Report Faults Election Official in Dodge City Polling Change," *Salina Journal*, February 26, 2020.

Smithsonian Institution. "The Machinery of Democracy," American History. si.edu., 2004.

Smithsonian Institution. "Voting and Electioneering, 1780–1899," Democracy Exhibit.

Somin, Ilya. *"Democracy and Political Ignorance: Why Smaller Government Is Smarter*, 2nd ed. Stanford: Stanford University Press, 2016.

Soros, Jonathan. "The Missing Right: A Constitutional Right to Vote," *Democracy*, Spring 2013, no. 28.

St. Louis County Board of Election Commissioners. "Biennial Report to the Public," 2012, 2014, 2016, 2018.

State of Nevada. "Nevada Election Laws," NRS–293.

Stromquist, Kat. "Election Gear on County's To-Do List," *Arkansas Democrat Gazette*, January 5, 2020.

Suttman-Lea, Mara. "Poll Worker Decision Making at the American Ballot Box," MIT Election Lab, July 11, 2019.

Taliesin, Julia. "Poll Workers Arrested in Medford," *Wicked Local*, November 6, 2019.

Tareen, Sophia. "Illinois' Automatic Voter Registration Delays Worry Experts," *APNews*, October 12, 2019.

Telford, Taylor. "Hackers Were Told to Break into U.S. Voting Machines. They Didn't Have Much Trouble," *Washington Post*, August 12, 2019.

Thompson, Nathan. "Rapid City Schools No Longer Election Sites," *Rapid City Journal*, November 3, 2019.

Tokaji, Daniel P. "The Right to Vote in an Age of Discontent," *Human Rights Magazine*, vol. 43, no. 2.

U.S. Election Assistance Commission. "2018 Election Administration and Voting Survey (EAVS)."

U.S. Election Assistance Commission. "EAVS Deep Dive: Election Technology," May 1, 2018.

U.S. Election Assistance Commission. "Ten Things to Know About Managing Aging Voting Systems," EAC.gov, October 14, 2017.

U.S. Senate Intelligence Committee. "Report of the Select Committee on Intelligence, United States Senate, on Russian Active Measures Campaigns and Interference in the 2016 U.S. Election," 2019.

University of Southern California. "Mapping America's Future: Four Ways GIS Data Impacts Elections," August 12, 2019.

University of Vermont Research Shop. "Ballot Order Effect," April 2, 2008.

Varner, Brian. "I Bought Used Voting Equipment on eBay for $100 Apiece. What I Found Was Alarming," *Wired*, October 25, 2018.

Vasilogambros, Matt. "Few People Want to Be Poll Workers, and That's a Problem," PewTrusts.org, October 22, 2018.

Vaughn, Monica, and Kathe Tanner. "Thousands of SLO County Voters Receive Two Ballots Weeks Before Election Day," *San Luis Obispo Tribune*, February 14, 2020.

Vedantam, Shankar. "Why the First Name on the Ballot Often Wins," NPR, July 27, 2016.

Vozzella, Laura. "The Teen who Messed Up His Absentee Ballot, Creating Virginia's Previous Tied Race," *Washington Post*, December 31, 2017.

Vozzella, Laura, and Ted Mellnik. "Va. Election Officials Assigned Twenty-Six Voters to the Wrong District. It Might've Cost Democrats a Pivotal Race," *Washington Post*, May 13, 2018.

Walker, Heather. "E-signatures in Elections: The Key to Preventing Voter Fraud?" Cryptomathic.com, October 16, 2016.

Wegmann, Philip. "Broward County's Election Office Is a National Disgrace," *Washington Examiner*, November 9, 2018.

Whittaker, Zack. "Top Voting Machine Maker Reverses Position on Election Security, Promises Paper Ballots," Tech Crunch, June 9, 2019.

Williams, Timothy. "First Came a Flood of Ballot Measures from Voters. Then Politicians Pushed Back," *New York Times*, October 15, 2018.

Wisconsin Elections Commission. "Authenticity of Ballots and Responsibility for Conducting Recounts," Administering Wisconsin's Election Laws, 2010.

Wood, Colin. "States Need to Improve for National GIS Infrastructure to Work, Report Says," StateScoop, January 3, 2020.

Index

About the Author

GLORIA SHUR BILCHIK IS AN ELECTION JUNKIE. She lives in Creve Coeur, Missouri, a suburb of St. Louis.

She has never run for office, but she admits to having fantasized about it. She has been a paid election-day poll worker, a campaign staffer in a Missouri state representative race, and coordinator of volunteers for the local office of a national presidential campaign (Obama '08). She has canvassed for local and statewide candidates, volunteered on voter registration drives and petition-gathering initiatives, and has helped compile and proofread information for voters' guides published by the League of Women Voters. She votes in almost every election.

She is married to Arthur Lieber, who ran for US Congress twice. Even when he's not on the ballot, the couple's election-night ritual is to follow returns obsessively, on multiple electronic devices. Bilchik shares America's collective outrage when elections seem unfair, and she mourns and gripes when the results do not go her way.

In her career as a freelance writer, she has gravitated to stories about voting and elections. She is the editor and a principal contributor to OccasionalPlanet.org, a political blog that gives voice to writers with progressive views.

THANK YOU FOR READING *Election Insiders* and sharing my journey into the inner workings of elections. If you have enjoyed the book, if you have questions, or if you would like to share your own experiences as a voter or an election worker, I would love to hear from you. Please contact me at ElectionInsiders@gmail.com.

Your feedback is important to me. I would enjoy reading any comments you might share on Amazon, Goodreads, LibraryThing or your favorite book site.

Gloria Shur Bilchik

Made in the USA
Middletown, DE
12 August 2020